THE
BEST
RECIPES
FROM
AMERICA'S
FOOD
FESTIVALS

JAMES O. FRAIOLI

ALPHA

A member of Penguin Group (USA) Inc.

ALPHA BOOKS

Published by the Penguin Group

Penguin Group (USA) Inc., 375 Hudson Street, New York, New York 10014, USA

Penguin Group (Canada), 90 Eglinton Avenue East, Suite 700, Toronto, Ontario M4P 2Y3, Canada (a division of Pearson Penguin Canada Inc.)

Penguin Books Ltd., 80 Strand, London WC2R 0RL, England

Penguin Ireland, 25 St. Stephen's Green, Dublin 2, Ireland (a division of Penguin Books Ltd.)

Penguin Group (Australia), 250 Camberwell Road, Camberwell, Victoria 3124, Australia (a division of Pearson Australia Group Pty. Ltd.)

Penguin Books India Pvt. Ltd., 11 Community Centre, Panchsheel Park, New Delhi—110 017, India

Penguin Group (NZ), 67 Apollo Drive, Rosedale, North Shore, Auckland 1311, New Zealand (a division of Pearson New Zealand Ltd.)

Penguin Books (South Africa) (Pty.) Ltd., 24 Sturdee Avenue, Rosebank, Johannesburg 2196, South Africa

Penguin Books Ltd., Registered Offices: 80 Strand, London WC2R 0RL, England

International Standard Book Number: 978-1-59257-664-7
Library of Congress Catalog Card Number: 2007924617

09 08 07   8 7 6 5 4 3 2 1

Interpretation of the printing code: The rightmost number of the first series of numbers is the year of the book's printing; the rightmost number of the second series of numbers is the number of the book's printing. For example, a printing code of 07-1 shows that the first printing occurred in 2007.

Printed in the United States of America

CONTENTS

PART 1: STARTERS, SNACKS, AND ACCENTS

PART 2: MAIN DISHES

MEAT AND POULTRY

SEAFOOD

PART 3: FRUITS, NUTS, AND VEGETABLES

PART 4: DESSERTS

APPENDIXES

INTRODUCTION

Welcome to an exciting book—part cookbook, part travelogue—that will take you across America to visit some of the best food festivals held annually throughout the country. And on the journey, you will discover a prized collection of delicious, mouthwatering recipes, all crafted by winning festival participants who are gracious enough to share their favorite dishes with you.

(Stockton Asparagus Festival)

Food festivals began to emerge in American cities and towns as far back as the early 1900s. They served to delight the palate and boost local economies, and at the same time pay tribute to new foods being introduced to the region.

One such famous food and festival made its mark in early American history: the delectable cherry. The early settlers brought this wonderful fruit, with its ruby-red color and tangy taste, to America in the 1600s.

Later, cherry trees became part of the gardens of French settlers as they established such cities as Detroit and other Midwestern settlements. In the mid-1800s, modern-day cherry production began, particularly in Michigan, where the climate proved to be ideal for growing cherries. By the early 1900s, the cherry industry was firmly established in Michigan, and production soon surpassed other major crops. To celebrate Michigan's explosive cherry harvest, a festival originated from a small spring ceremony known as the "Blessing of the Blossoms." Eventually, the celebration grew to what is better known today as the National Cherry Festival in Traverse City, Michigan—the Cherry Capital of the World. Every July, the National Cherry Festival puts on a grand event, welcoming thousands of cherry lovers to celebrate Michigan's luscious fruit and to dine on endless cherries in a vast array of dishes.

(*National Cherry Festival*)

Like Michigan's National Cherry Festival, many of America's food festivals have a similar history. Whether it's the cherries from Michigan, the catfish from Mississippi, or the peanuts from Alabama, food festivals celebrate and promote the arrival of a particular harvest or a state's culinary specialty.

Food festivals also represent community pride, reflected by the hundreds—often thousands—of visitors who join festival volunteers and representatives to pay tribute to the state's featured food while raising funds to support local schools, churches, charities, and other community organizations.

Like the food itself, American food festivals come in all sizes, colors, and shapes. Some festivals are one- or two-day affairs that are free of charge and orchestrated on a rural street or behind a restaurant or local church—more of a local party than a food festival. One such festival is the National Hot Dog Festival in Columbus, Ohio, which happens to be home to the World's Longest Hot Dog, according to the *Guinness Book of World Records*. At this festival, a handful of residents gather in July for the chance to participate in a hot dog eating contest and a hot dog cooking contest—and sample plenty of mouthwatering hot dogs—while strolling through the festival's classic car show and listening to live music.

Other food festivals, meanwhile, are designed to become extravagant gala affairs that consume city block after city block and last anywhere from 3 to 10 days, drawing tens of thousands of gourmands from across the globe. In fact, many of these notable food festivals are the headline attraction in their state, where visitor attendance and revenue far surpass any sporting event or museum in town. Case in point: the Gilroy Garlic Festival, one of the largest food festivals in the United States, held annually in Gilroy, California. On average, the Gilroy Garlic Festival attracts more than 125,000 people, who arrive in droves to sample such diverse creations as garlic ice cream and garlic french fries. Attendees can also enjoy multiple stages filled with musical entertainment, a Great Garlic Cook-Off, celebrity cooking demonstrations, a children's play area, arts and crafts, and many interactive displays. A Queen of Garlic is also crowned yearly. More than 4,000 volunteers from over 160 nonprofit groups make the Gilroy Garlic Festival possible. It's reported that more than 3 million people have attended the festival since its inception in 1979.

(Gilroy Garlic Festival)

Like the National Hot Dog Festival or the Gilroy Garlic Festival, American food festivals often feature much more than just food. While attending a festival, expect to find parades; fitness runs; competitive races; car shows; beauty pageants; the crowning of a festival queen; arts and crafts booths; food-related products for sale; and plenty of cook-offs, bake-offs, and eating contest opportunities.

So what are you waiting for? Turn the page and begin your gastronomic journey into the culinary world of America's food festivals. You'll discover a long list of award-winning recipes guaranteed to make you smile along the way.

ACKNOWLEDGMENTS

I would like to thank my acquisitions editor, Paul Dinas at Alpha Books; Nadine Saubers for her outstanding research assistance; all the food festivals who kindly contributed to this book; my literary agent, Andrea Hurst; and my wife, Cindy, for her continued support.

Part 1

Starters, Snacks, and Accents

KONA COFFEE CULTURAL FESTIVAL

Kona, Hawaii
November
808-326-7820
www.konacoffeefest.com

The annual Kona Coffee Cultural Festival, Hawaii's oldest food festival and the only coffee festival in the United States, is celebrating 180 years of coffee tradition on the picture-perfect island of Kona. During the 10-day event held every November, 18,000 visitors enjoy more than 50 festival events, including coffee tastings, parades, a Miss Kona Coffee Pageant, farm tours, art exhibits, an international marketplace, outdoor concerts, a golf tournament, and exciting Kona coffee competitions.

Watch as competing baristas go cup-to-cup during the Kona Signature Cup. The competition showcases Hawaii's talented baristas in a lively, timed event as they set out to create the best original beverage featuring Kona coffee. A panel of four judges critique each drink based on presentation, preparation, taste, and appearance. The public can also vote for their favorite barista.

Another festival contest worth catching is the Kona Coffee Picking Contest, which attracts coffee pickers of all levels of experience. Visitors and residents alike have the opportunity to tour the palatial coffee farms that serve as stunning backdrops as competitors try their hand at picking only the reddest Kona coffee cherries during a 3-minute competition.

During the festival's Cupping Competition, local coffee farms submit a 50-pound sample of their best coffee. To be eligible, the coffee submitted must have been harvested in Kona. Unlike the other competitions, this signature event is a blind tasting. The coffee samples, both green and roasted, are placed on a table for the judges to independently evaluate. The judges reward high marks for fragrance, aroma, taste, nose, aftertaste, and body.

Follow these tips for making the perfect cup of Kona coffee, from the Kona Coffee Cultural Festival's website, and someday you, too, might be entering a competition at the Kona Coffee Cultural Festival:

- The best brewing method is an automatic drip system with a paper filter.
- Use fresh, cold water.
- Add 1 tablespoon Kona coffee per 6 ounces water. For peak flavor, keep the brewed coffee warm and consume within 1 hour.
- For iced Kona coffee, brew slightly stronger. Cool to room temperature before pouring over ice.
- After you've opened a bag of Kona coffee, seal it tightly and store it in the refrigerator.

Kona coffee was first planted in Kona in 1828, and coffee and Kona became a perfect match—Kona with its rich volcanic soil, hardworking family farmers, and perfect climatic conditions. Today, Kona coffee is one of Hawaii's most economically successful crops. Many of the Kona farmers tending the plantations today are proud to be fifth-generation coffee farmers, continuing the tradition and honoring their heritage with every harvest.

(Kona Coffee Cultural Festival)

Pork Florentine Pinwheels with Tropical Kona Coffee Sauce

Adapted from the recipe by Barbara Housel

Yield: 6 to 8 servings

Tropical Kona Coffee Sauce:

1½ cups beef stock

2 cloves garlic, sliced

1 tsp. Dijon mustard

4 Hawaiian chili peppers (optional)

1 cup strong Kiele O Kona coffee

1 TB. lilikoi juice, guava juice, or passion-orange juice

1 cup pineapple juice

2 TB. honey

¼ cup chardonnay

1 to 3 TB. butter

1 tsp. cornstarch mixed with 1 cup coffee

Stuffing:

2 TB. butter

½ cup chopped red onions

¼ cup mushrooms, chopped

1 tsp. minced garlic

½ cup dried summer savory

½ tsp. dried basil

Salt and fresh ground black pepper

3 TB. heavy cream

½ cup artichoke hearts, drained and coarsely chopped

2 cups spinach, cooked, drained, and chopped

2 TB. fresh parsley, chopped

¼ cup toasted macadamia nuts, chopped

¼ cup breadcrumbs

1½ lb. pork loin

3 TB. balsamic vinegar

1. *Tropical Kona Coffee Sauce:* In a small saucepan, combine beef stock, garlic, mustard, chili peppers, Kona coffee, lilikoi juice, pineapple juice, and balsamic vinegar. Cook about 5 minutes or until mixture reduces by ½. Strain and return liquid to the saucepan.

2. Add honey and chardonnay, and cook for a few minutes. Whisk in 1 to 3 tablespoons butter, thicken with cornstarch, and keep warm. If sauce becomes too thick, add a little more coffee.

3. *Stuffing:* Heat 2 tablespoons butter in a large skillet, add onions, and sauté until soft. Add mushrooms and sauté until soft. Add garlic, summer savory, basil, salt, and pepper, and cook several minutes, stirring frequently. Add heavy cream, artichoke hearts, and spinach, and cook 2 minutes or until cream evaporates. Remove from heat and add parsley, nuts, and enough breadcrumbs to tighten mixture. Allow to cool.

4. Preheat the oven to 375°F.

5. Slice pork into ½-inch rounds and place between 2 pieces of plastic wrap. Pound with a meat mallet until roughly ¼-inch thick. Season meat with salt and pepper. Stuff with stuffing and roll up pork loin. Secure with toothpicks if necessary.

6. In a heavy, ovenproof skillet, brown meat on all sides. Place the skillet in the oven for 12 minutes to finish cooking. Remove from oven and allow to rest.

7. To serve, slice pork into rounds, remove toothpicks, plate, and serve with sauce. Good served with mashed potatoes, carrots, broccoli, or salad greens.

Kona Coffee Bread Pudding

Adapted from the recipe by Barbara Kossow

---

5 TB. instant Kona Coffee

2 cups cream

12 TB. or ¾ cup butter

1¾ cups sugar

5 eggs, beaten

2½ cups regular or whole milk

5 TB. cornstarch

¼ tsp. salt

1 tsp. vanilla extract (optional)

¾ loaf Punaluu Sweet Bread, cubed

Cinnamon sugar (optional)

---

1. Preheat the oven to 350°F.

2. In a small bowl, mix 1 tablespoon coffee with cream.

3. In a saucepan over medium heat, melt butter. Add 1 cup sugar and coffee cream, and mix well. Set aside to cool.

4. When mixture is cool, add eggs and stir well. Set aside.

5. In another small bowl, mix remaining 4 tablespoons coffee with milk.

6. In a saucepan over medium heat, mix remaining ¾ cup sugar, cornstarch, and salt. Gradually blend in milk mixture. Cook 1 or 2 minutes or until mixture thickens, stirring to prevent burning.

7. When mixture has cooled slightly, add vanilla extract (if using).

8. Arrange bread in a single layer on the bottom of a baking pan. Cover bread with pudding mixture.

9. Stir egg mixture before adding to pudding and bread. Use a fork to lightly incorporate wet mixture with bread.

10. Top bread with desired fruit, raisins, coconut, plums, or other dried fruit. Bake for 30 to 45 minutes. Sprinkle with cinnamon sugar when hot (if using).

Mika's Coffee Surprise

Adapted from the recipe by Mika Bettencourt

---

200 g dark chocolate	⅔ cup unsalted butter
1 TB. strong Kona coffee	¾ cup almond or hazelnut meal
1 TB. 100% Kona Gold liqueur	5 eggs, separated
⅔ cup superfine sugar	Chocolate icing

---

1. Preheat the oven to 350°F. Grease and flour a 10-inch round cake pan.

2. Place chocolate, coffee, liqueur, sugar, and butter in a heatproof bowl. Set over a pan of simmering water until chocolate and butter have melted. Remove from heat, and stir until combined.

3. Add almond meal and mix well.

4. Using a handheld mixer on medium speed, beat in egg yolks, one at time.

5. In a separate bowl, beat egg whites until soft peaks form. Stir a couple spoonfuls into chocolate mixture to lighten it before gently folding in the rest.

6. Pour batter into the prepared pan, and bake for 40 minutes or until a toothpick or cake tester inserted into the center comes out clean.

7. Cool in the pan before removing. Pour chocolate sauce over top of sliced cake for decoration.

NATIONAL CORNBREAD FESTIVAL

South Pittsburg, Tennessee
April
423-837-0022
www.nationalcornbread.com

Every April in downtown South Pittsburg, Tennessee, the National Cornbread Festival brings cast iron and cornbread together. Sponsored by Martha White and Lodge Cast Iron, the festival's claim to fame is the cook-off, where the challenge of the day is who can make the best main dish cornbread recipe prepared with at least 1 cup Martha White Cornmeal or 1 package Martha White Cornbread Mix. The winning cornbread must also be cooked in Lodge cast-iron cookware.

Martha White is a trusted staple in kitchens across the South, and has been for more than 100 years. In 1899, Richard Lindsey named his company's finest flour after his 3-year-old daughter, Martha. Since then, Martha White Foods has been producing quality grain-based products, including flour, cornmeal, grits, and baking mixes. Today, Southern cooks rely on Martha White for easy-to-bake foods with down-home flavor.

While attending the National Cornbread Festival, every visitor is guaranteed a cornbread education. For instance, do you know the difference between white and yellow cornmeal? The answer is in the color of corn used. The varying cornmeal colors are interchangeable in recipes. Historically, white cornmeal is preferred in the South while yellow cornmeal is popular in Texas and the rest of the United States.

Aside from the highly publicized cook-offs, the festival boasts hundreds of activities for attendees—local arts and crafts, clown and car shows, a carnival, puppeteers, trolley rides, and a 5K fitness race. Endless samples of award-winning cornbread treats are always an arm's reach away down "Cornbread Alley." It's here where you can enjoy southern cornbread at its finest while walking away with recipe cards on how to make these divine delicacies in the comfort of your own home.

(National Cornbread Festival)

Monte Cristo Cornbread Skillet Supper

Adapted from the recipe by Janice Elder

Yield: 4 servings

---

1 (6-oz.) pkg. Martha White Cotton Pickin' or Buttermilk Cornbread Mix

1½ cups chopped cooked turkey

½ cup chopped cooked ham

1½ cups shredded Swiss cheese

4 eggs

1 cup milk

2 TB. mayonnaise

2 TB. honey mustard

1½ tsp. salt

½ tsp. pepper

½ cup currant jelly

Confectioners' sugar

---

1. Prepare cornbread mix according to package directions, except bake in a 10½-inch Lodge cast-iron skillet. Cornbread will be thin.

2. Remove cornbread from the skillet, cool, and cut into cubes. Wipe out the skillet with paper towels and grease generously. Place cornbread cubes back in the skillet. Top with turkey, ham, and shredded cheese.

3. Preheat the oven to 350°F.

4. In a medium bowl, whisk together eggs, milk, mayonnaise, 1 tablespoon honey mustard, salt, and pepper until well blended. Pour evenly over ingredients in the skillet. Bake for 30 to 35 minutes or until set and lightly browned.

5. Meanwhile, in a small saucepan over medium-low heat, warm currant jelly slightly to melt. Add remaining 1 tablespoon honey mustard, and whisk to blend.

6. Remove the skillet from the oven. Cut mixture into wedges, sprinkle with confectioners' sugar, and serve with currant jelly and mustard sauce.

Grilled Chicken Skillet Pizza with Cornmeal Crust

Adapted from the recipe by Barbara Estabrook

Yield: 4 servings

1 (14-oz.) can chicken broth (1¾ cups)	3 or 4 thin slices red onion, cut in half
1 tsp. dried Montreal chicken seasoning	½ cup diced red bell pepper
¼ tsp. salt	1 small zucchini, halved lengthwise and thinly sliced
1 cup Martha White Plain Yellow Cornmeal	⅓ cup marinara sauce
3 TB. butter	1 (6-oz.) pkg. cooked grilled chicken strips, chopped (about 1 cup)
1 egg, slightly beaten	
3 TB. shredded Parmesan and Romano cheese	½ cup chopped button mushrooms
	1 cup shredded Fontina cheese
1 TB. olive oil	

1. Preheat the oven to 375°F.

2. In a 3-quart saucepan, combine broth, seasoning, and salt, and bring to a boil. Remove from heat and gradually stir in cornmeal. Add butter, egg, and Parmesan and Romano cheese, and stir until well blended. Set aside.

3. In a 12-inch Lodge cast-iron skillet, heat olive oil over medium-high heat. Add onion, bell pepper, and zucchini, and cook, stirring frequently, for 3 to 5 minutes or until onions are lightly browned. Spoon into a bowl and set aside.

4. Cool the skillet slightly, wipe it clean with paper towels, and spray the bottom only with nonstick cooking spray. Spoon cornmeal mixture into the skillet. With oiled hands, press down evenly in the bottom and ¼ inch up the sides to form crust.

5. Spread marinara over crust, and top with vegetable mixture, chicken, mushrooms, and Fontina cheese. Bake for 23 to 25 minutes or until golden brown along the edge. Loosen edges with a knife, cool 10 minutes, and cut into wedges.

Beefy Cornhusker Pizza

Adapted from the recipe by Emily Gill

Yield: 6 to 8 servings

---

3 TB. butter-flavored Crisco

1½ cups Martha White Self-Rising Cornmeal Mix

1 TB. Martha White Self-Rising Flour

¼ cup water

1 cup buttermilk

¾ cup Ragu Pizza Sauce

1 lb. 90 percent lean ground beef, browned

2 cups shredded Colby Jack cheese

---

1. Preheat the oven to 450°F.

2. Add Crisco to a 12-inch Lodge cast-iron skillet and place in the oven to warm.

3. In a large mixing bowl, combine cornmeal mix, flour, water, and buttermilk. Pour into the preheated skillet. Spoon pizza sauce over cornmeal mixture. Sprinkle with browned ground beef, and top with shredded cheese.

4. Bake for 20 to 25 minutes or until golden brown.

Mile-High Greens and Creamy Cornbread Skillet

Adapted from the recipe by Janine Washle

Yield: 8 servings

1 cup Martha White Plain Yellow Cornmeal

1 TB. butter

1 cup boiling water

1 egg, beaten

1 cup milk or buttermilk

½ tsp. salt

1 TB. baking powder

1 TB. Martha White All-Purpose Flour

1 cup shredded mozzarella cheese

1½ TB. Crisco or canola oil

1 onion, chopped

2 cups chopped cooked ham

1 lb. kale, trimmed, rinsed, and chopped

1 lb. mustard or turnip greens, trimmed, rinsed, and chopped

½ cup roasted red peppers, sliced into strips

Salt and pepper

1 tsp. hot pepper sauce (optional)

1. Preheat the oven to 450°F. Grease a 12-inch Lodge cast-iron skillet.

2. In a medium bowl, combine cornmeal and butter. Gradually stir in boiling water until blended and butter is melted. Stir in egg.

3. Gradually stir in milk, and continue to stir constantly. Add salt, baking powder, flour, and cheese, and stir until blended. Pour mixture into the prepared skillet, and bake for 15 to 20 minutes or until set or lightly browned.

4. Meanwhile, in a Lodge cast-iron Dutch oven, heat Crisco over medium-high heat. Add onion and cook until tender. Add ham and cook until browned.

5. Spoon ham mixture over cornbread, leaving 1 inch uncovered around the edge. Return Dutch oven to heat and add kale and mustard greens in 3 or 4 additions as they wilt down. Stir in roasted red peppers. Cook for 5 to 7 minutes or until greens change to dark green.

6. Stir in salt, pepper, and hot pepper sauce (if using). Spoon greens over ham layer. Loosely tent with foil, and bake for 10 to 15 minutes or until hot. To serve, cut into wedges with a long, sharp knife.

Loaded Potato Cornbread

Adapted from the recipe by Shania Davis

Yield: 8 servings

1 TB. vegetable shortening	½ cup mashed potatoes
1 cup Martha White Self-Rising Cornmeal Mix	¼ cup crumbled bacon bits
1 TB. Martha White flour	1¼ cups buttermilk
1 TB. onion flakes	½ cup grated cheddar cheese
1 tsp. sugar	

1. Preheat the oven to 425°F.

2. Add vegetable shortening to an 8-inch Lodge cast-iron skillet and place in the oven to warm.

3. In a bowl, combine cornmeal mix, flour, onion flakes, and sugar. Pour melted vegetable shortening over dry ingredients. Add mashed potatoes and bacon bits, and stir to combine. Add buttermilk and mix.

4. Pour ½ of batter in the skillet and sprinkle with ½ of cheese. Pour in remaining batter, and top with remaining cheese.

5. Bake for 40 minutes or until brown.

ROSENDALE INTERNATIONAL PICKLE FESTIVAL

Rosendale, New York
November
845-658-9649
www.picklefest.com

During a simple "pickle party" thrown in a neighborhood backyard in 1998, Rosendale International Pickle Festival founders Bill and Cathy Brooks agreed that if they could host a similar party—this time for a larger audience while introducing visitors to the fun and excitement of pickles and all things pickled—a pickle festival could take off. The Brooks family's dream couldn't have been closer to the truth.

With the support of the Rosendale Chamber of Commerce, the Brooks family launched the first pickle festival. They hoped the celebrated pickle would draw in at least a couple hundred attendees. Their initial goal was to expand visitors' culinary horizons while tempting them with wonderful exhibitions showcasing the international cultures and customs through the simple but alluring pickle. Unbeknownst to the Brooks family, more than 1,000 pickle enthusiasts showed up! Who knew pickles were so popular?

The following year, 1999, German pickles and pickling traditions were introduced to the festival and attendance doubled to more than 2,000. A roaming accordionist, strolling musicians, and Shupplattler Dancers added to the festival festivities. The next year, the famous Vlasic Pickle Company lent their support, along with offering guests plenty of free tastings, a Pickle Juice Drinking Contest, a Pickle Eating Contest, and a Pickle Toss.

Today, the pickle festival has gone international, as it often receives inquiries from as far away as India, Bosnia, and Lebanon. The festival grounds have also expanded, now consuming more than 12,000 square feet of vendors; more than 5,000 pickle fans; and endless tasty pickle treats such as cucumber pickles; pickled peppers, tomatoes, okra, asparagus, and beans; deep-fried pickles; and pickle pizza.

(Rosendale International Pickle Festival)

Bread and Butter Pickles

Adapted from the recipe by Judith Charles

Yield: 8 pints

4 qt. medium cucumbers, sliced	3 cups cider vinegar
6 medium white onions, sliced (6 cups)	1½ tsp. turmeric
2 green bell peppers, sliced (1⅔ cups)	1½ tsp. celery seed
3 cloves garlic	2 TB. mustard seed
⅓ cup granulated pickling salt	Salt
5 cups sugar	

1. In a small cooking pot, combine cucumbers, onions, bell peppers, and whole garlic. Add pickling salt, cover with cracked ice, mix thoroughly, and let stand approximately 3 hours.

2. Drain well and remove garlic. Add sugar, cider vinegar, turmeric, celery seed, mustard seed, salt, and pepper. Bring the contents of the pot to a boil.

3. Meanwhile, have ready hot canning jars with lids. (Cool jars will often crack when submerged into boiling water.)

4. After contents boil, fill the jars to ½ inch from the top. Seal with the lids.

5. Process the jars in a boiling water bath for about 5 minutes (start timing when water returns to boil).

Rick's Picks Dill Pickles

Adapted from the recipe by pickler Rick Field

Yield: 6 pint jars of pickles, about 4 pounds

18 dill heads or 6 TB. dill seed and several fronds dill leaf

24 cloves garlic, peeled and halved

6 TB. pickling spice

36 whole black peppercorns

3 cups water

3 cups vinegar

6 tsp. kosher salt

4 lb. pickling cucumbers, washed

1. In each of 6 pint jars, add 3 dill heads or 1 tablespoon dill seed and several fronds dill leaf, 4 cloves garlic, 1 tablespoon pickling spice, and 6 whole black peppercorns. Set jars aside.

2. In a large pan over medium-high heat, add water, vinegar, and kosher salt. Bring to a boil. You might need more of this mixture and should have extra on hand. Also, be sure to have liquid at a roaring boil when placing mixture in the jars.

3. Pack washed cucumbers tightly into jars, and ladle in mixture, leaving ½-inch headroom. Seal with the lids. Place the jars immediately in the boiling water bath. Process for 7 minutes.

4. Tighten the lids, but do not overtighten. The lid is good if it doesn't "pop" when you press down on it the next day.

Grandma's Pickled Tomatoes

Adapted from the recipe by Cathy Brooks

---

30 to 36 small green tomatoes

6 celery stalks, chopped

1 green or red bell pepper, seeds and ribs removed and sliced

1 onion, sliced

1 garlic clove, sliced

2 qt. vinegar

1 sprig dill

2 qt. water

1 cup salt

---

1. Distribute tomatoes, celery, bell pepper slices, onion slices, and garlic slices among canning jars and pack well.

2. In a large saucepan over medium-high heat, add vinegar, dill, water, and salt. Bring to a boil, pour liquid over tomatoes in jars, and place a piece of dill on top.

3. Seal the jars and turn upside down for 24 hours. Pickled tomatoes should be ready to eat in about 2 months.

MUSHROOM FESTIVAL

Kennett Square, Pennsylvania
September
1-888-440-9920
www.mushroomfestival.org

Kennett Square, Pennsylvania, is considered by many to be the "The Mushroom Capital of the World." There are more mushroom-growing operations here than any other area in the United States. More than 100,000 visitors come from far and wide to experience this "small-town America" festival.

Thanks to a hardworking group of 300+ fun-loving enthusiastic volunteers, the Mushroom Festival guarantees an experience like no other. Its mission: to promote the mushroom, educate consumers about the health benefits of mushrooms, and promote tourism in Southern Chester County—all while financially supporting local and regional charities. Recently, *Travelocity* voted the Mushroom Festival one of the top 10 festivals in Pennsylvania. The famous festival has also debuted on the Food Network's *All American Festival* show.

While attending the Mushroom Festival, visitors will appreciate the excitement that abounds inside the Culinary Tent. It's here where some incredible mushroom cooking demonstrations take place. Whether you're a novice in the kitchen or an experienced chef, the festival's cooking demonstrations provide plenty of useful tips on a collection of mushroom dishes from featured chefs. Also inside the Culinary Tent are educational booths that share nutritional facts about the mushroom, along with the different varieties and how to use them in everyday cooking.

For the really enthusiastic mushroom lovers, the festival offers a Mushroom Soup Cook-Off for Amateurs, where the winning mushroom soup fetches $500. There's also a Mushroom Judging Contest for the top growers in the country who can produce prize-winning mushrooms.

Other exciting activities include private Mushroom Farm Tours, where visitors can observe the entire growing process firsthand, live music, mushroom growing exhibits, classic car shows, parades, auctions, and plenty of children's activities.

(Mushroom Festival)

Kennett Square
Cream of Mushroom Soup

Adapted from the recipe by Shannon Bellafiore

4 TB. olive oil	6 cups chicken broth
4 TB. butter	8 tsp. flour
1 cup shallots, minced	1½ cups sherry
44 oz. sliced Kennett Square Mushroom Medley or 6 oz. portobello, 6 oz. crimini, 8 oz. shiitake, 4 oz. oyster, and 20 oz. button mushrooms	1 tsp. thyme
	2 tsp. salt
	1 tsp. white pepper
8 oz. dried porcini	1 cup heavy cream

1. In a large stockpot, add olive oil and butter. Heat over high heat until fully melted, about 1 minute. Add shallots and sauté about 2 minutes. Reduce heat to medium, add Mushroom Medley and porcini mushrooms, and cook about 20 minutes. Add 4 cups chicken stock, and cook about 10 minutes.

2. Remove 3 cups mushrooms. Place in a blender with remaining 2 cups chicken broth, and purée about 2 minutes or until desired consistency. For a smoother soup with no chunks, purée all mushrooms. Add mushroom purée back to the stockpot with original mushrooms.

3. In separate bowl, whisk flour into 1 cup sherry. Slowly stir into soup.

4. Add thyme, salt, white pepper, and heavy cream to soup, and cook for 5 minutes.

5. Add remaining ½ cup sherry, cook for 10 minutes, and serve.

Big Sam's Crab and Mushroom Soup

Adapted from the recipe by Samuel V. Onizuk

½ cup butter

½ cup onion, chopped

1 TB. garlic, chopped

2 lb. mixed mushrooms, sliced

1 TB. Old Bay seasoning

2 TB. parsley flakes

1 TB. Worcestershire sauce

1 qt. water

1 (14-oz.) can evaporated milk

4 to 6 large crusty rolls (for soup "bowls")

½ lb. lump crabmeat

½ cup red bell pepper, diced

2 TB. sweet sherry

---

1. In a 4-quart stockpot over medium-high heat, melt butter. Add onion and garlic, and cook, stirring occasionally, for 5 minutes. Stir in mushrooms, Old Bay, 1 tablespoon parsley flakes, and Worcestershire sauce. Cook 5 minutes. Add water and milk, and simmer, uncovered, for 15 minutes.

2. Meanwhile, cut tops off rolls and hollow them out to make soup bowls, reserving some bread.

3. Break reserved bread into small pieces and stir into soup, 1 cup at a time, until soup is sufficiently thick. Add crabmeat, red bell pepper, and sherry. Adjust seasoning to taste.

4. Ladle soup into bread bowls, and top with remaining 1 tablespoon parsley flakes.

Zuppone di Funge e Potate (Mushroom and Potato Soup)

Adapted from the recipe by Marie E. Boulden

Yield: 6 to 8 portions

¾ cup butter	6 cloves garlic, minced
2 medium yellow onions, chopped	4 thin slices Italian bread
6 large Yukon gold potatoes, peeled, boiled, and cubed	16 oz. mixed mushrooms, sliced
1 (32-oz.) can chicken broth	½ cup roasted red peppers from a jar, chopped
1 cup heavy cream	Salt and pepper
1 cup freshly grated Parmesan cheese	

1. In large stockpot over medium-high heat, melt ¼ cup butter. Add onions and sauté about 5 minutes or until onions are translucent. Add potatoes, stir in chicken broth, and reduce heat to medium. Cover and simmer 20 minutes. Add cream and Parmesan cheese.

2. In a large sauté pan over medium-high heat, melt remaining ½ cup butter. Add garlic and sauté 1 minute. Add bread slices and sauté until crisp and brown on both sides. Remove bread and set aside.

3. Add mushrooms to the sauté pan, and cook until slightly brown and fragrant. Stir in roasted red peppers. Stir mushroom mixture into soup, and season with salt and pepper.

4. Ladle soup into bowls. Top with Italian bread slices and a little grated Parmesan cheese.

Smoky Mushroom Basil Bisque

Adapted from the recipe by Lisa Grant

2 TB. olive oil

16 oz. fresh sliced white mushrooms, coarsely chopped

2 TB. flour

2 oz. diced prosciutto

2 cups chicken stock or broth

2 cups half-and-half

⅓ cup chopped fresh basil

1 cup shredded smoked Gouda cheese

Fresh ground pepper

4 sprigs basil

1. Heat olive oil in a large, heavy saucepan over medium-high heat. Add mushrooms and sauté until mushrooms are very tender, about 7 to 9 minutes.

2. Sprinkle mushrooms with flour, and stir well for 2 minutes. Add prosciutto. Gradually mix in stock. Bring to a simmer, stirring frequently.

3. Reduce heat to low and add half-and-half. Cook for about 10 minutes or until mixture thickens, stirring occasionally. Add chopped basil and cheese. Cook for another few minutes, and stir until cheese is melted.

4. Season soup with fresh ground pepper, ladle into bowls, and garnish with basil sprigs.

Mushroom and Oyster Croustades

Adapted from the recipe by Christine Coon

Yield: 24 servings

24 slices rye bread	1 cup heavy cream
3 TB. melted butter	1 TB. lemon juice
5 slices thick bacon, finely diced	1 cup shredded Jarlsberg cheese
1 lb. mixed mushrooms, chopped	1 doz. shucked oysters, coarsely chopped (about 1 cup)
5 scallions, finely diced	
⅓ cup sherry	Freshly ground pepper
	Paprika

---

1. Preheat the oven to 350°F.

2. Roll bread slices flat with a rolling pin and cut out a 3-inch circle from each slice. Brush one side of each circle with butter and press each, buttered side down, into a mini muffin cup. Bake for 7 minutes or until lightly toasted. Set aside.

3. Sauté bacon in a large skillet until crisp. Remove and drain on paper towels. Leave 2 tablespoons bacon fat in the pan. Add mushrooms and scallions, and sauté for 5 minutes. Add sherry and cook until most of liquid has evaporated. Add cream and cook for 5 minutes.

4. Add bacon, lemon juice, cheese, and oysters to the pan. Cook until cheese is melted, about 2 minutes. Season with freshly ground pepper and paprika, and remove from the stove.

5. Fill each bread cup ¾ full with mushroom mixture. Bake for 10 or 12 minutes or until set and just browned. Cool a few minutes, remove from muffin tins, and serve.

Smoked Portobello "Cappuccino"

Adapted from the recipe by Sandy Ciarrocchi

---

1 TB. olive oil	¼ lb. white mushrooms, sliced
1 clove garlic, minced	¼ cup dry sherry
¼ cup chopped onion	1½ cups chicken stock or broth
¼ cup chopped carrot	1½ cups heavy cream
¼ cup chopped celery	3 sprigs fresh thyme
6 oz. smoked portobello mushrooms, chopped*	Salt and pepper

---

1. Heat olive oil in a large saucepan over medium heat. Add garlic, onion, carrot, and celery, and cook until soft. Add portobello and white mushrooms, and cook until soft.

2. Deglaze pan with sherry, stirring to scrape browned bits free. Reduce heat to low heat and simmer for 10 minutes. Add stock, cream, and thyme.

3. Purée soup in a blender or food processor. Return purée to the pan, raise the heat to medium, and bring to a boil. Reduce heat to low and simmer until reduced to desired consistency.

4. Season with salt and pepper. Serve in cappuccino cups for an elegant flair.

*Smoked portobello mushrooms are available at specialty food stores. If unavailable, you can also smoke your own or use portobello mushrooms and add Liquid Smoke to taste.

SPAMARAMA FESTIVAL

Austin, Texas
April
512-834-1827
www.spamarama.org

The highly celebrated SPAMARAMA, held every year in Austin, Texas, welcomes visitors from across the country to plenty of festival fun, food, and excitement involving America's favorite canned meat—SPAM.

Long before the invention of computers and e-mail, Hormel Foods Corporation welcomed the world to SPAM, a precooked canned meat that continues to take America by storm. Consisting of chopped pork shoulder with ham meat added, along with salt, water, and sugar, SPAM has gained a peculiar infamy—along with something of a place in pop culture—and has even entered into folklore and urban legend. As of 1997, it is estimated that more than 5 billion cans of SPAM had been sold worldwide.

Based on *SPAMARAMA: The Cookbook* by David Dryden Arnsberger and John Booher, Austin's famous SPAM festival—SPAMARAMA—was introduced in the early spring of 1976 when two gentlemen fraternizing one afternoon bellyached about how chili cook-offs had become so commonplace. They agreed that if someone could make SPAM edible, that would be a challenge. As a result of that illustrious day, SPAMARAMA was born, making it, along with its famous SPAM-off, the first and longest-running SPAM event in the country. Today, more than 30 years later, SPAMARAMA is still going strong, while the featured SPAM Cook-Off now consists of two divisions: Open and Professional. Both events continue to enjoy notoriety from multiple site visits by the Food Network.

In addition to the top three prizes in each Cook-Off Division, the contestants—chefs, local restaurants and caterers, as well as self-proclaimed SPAM gourmets—battle to take home the coveted prize, the SPAMERICA Cup trophy, a "traveling" trophy with the previous winners' names emblazoned on the front. At the other extreme, there are always a few entrants going purely for the "Worst of Show" trophy.

If cooking isn't your forte, perhaps entering the SPAMALYMPICS is for you. Your imagination is your only limit when you compete in events such as the SPAM Disc Shoot, the SPAM Call (remotely similar to a hog call), the SPAM Can Relay, and the SPAMBURGER Eating Contest.

(*SPAMARAMA Festival*)

SPAM Chili Rellenos

Adapted from the recipe by Kelley Dooley (in memoriam) and David Cross

Yield: 6 to 8

8 large fresh Anaheim chilies	2 TB. cold water
Monterey Jack cheese, as needed (or 1 block)	1¼ tsp. salt
	1 TB. chopped cilantro
1 (12-oz.) can SPAM luncheon meat	1 cup sour cream
12 tomatillos, blanched and peeled	2 cups flour
2 to 4 medium serrano peppers, stems removed	3 eggs, separated
1½ cups chicken broth	1 TB. water
1 TB. cornstarch	Canola oil for frying

1. Poke a small hole at each end of Anaheims. Using either an outdoor grill or your oven broiler, roast Anaheims until charred on all sides. Immediately place Anaheims in a paper bag and close the top. After 10 minutes, remove Anaheims and peel burnt skin, which should easily slide off. Cut a small slit in the middle of Anaheims and gently remove seeds.

2. Slice cheese and SPAM into sticks a little shorter than Anaheims. Place an even number of SPAM and cheese slices into each Anaheim. Set aside.

3. In a medium saucepan over medium heat, boil tomatillos and serranos in broth for 7 to 10 minutes.

4. In a small bowl, dissolve cornstarch in cold water and add to boiling mixture along with 1 teaspoon salt and cilantro. Boil for 5 more minutes.

5. Remove sauce from heat and add to a blender. Blend until smooth, and strain seeds and fibers. Let sauce cool for 5 minutes, add sour cream, and stir until smooth.

6. Spoon Sour Cream Tomatillo Sauce in stuffed Anaheims, and close with a toothpick, slightly tapping the edges to hold the contents inside. Roll each Anaheim in flour and set aside.

7. In a medium bowl, beat egg whites until soft peaks form.

8. In a separate bowl, beat yolks with 1 tablespoon water and remaining ¼ teaspoon salt. Add flour a little at a time until mixture is creamy. Fold yolk mixture into whites.

9. Heat 2 inches canola oil in a wide frying pan over medium heat. Dip stuffed Anaheims into egg batter and slide into hot oil. When bottoms are golden brown, gently turn, using a spatula and fork, and cook the other side 3 or 4 minutes. Drain Anaheims on a paper towel. After cooling a few minutes (do not let them get cold!) ladle warm Sour Cream Tomatillo Sauce over Anaheims and serve.

Judge's Form

Name of Recipe

Entrant's Name

SPAM Tenderloin Kebobs with SPAM and Grilled Corn Chorizo

Adapted from the recipe by David Spooner

Yield: 2 servings

4 pieces green bell pepper, cut into 1-in. cubes

6 pieces pineapple, cut into 1-in. cubes

1 (12-oz.) can SPAM luncheon meat, cut into 4 medallions

1 cup yellow corn, grilled on the cob

1 oz. chorizo, cut into slices

3 tricolor bell peppers (green, orange, yellow, or red), chopped

1 (12-oz.) can Smoked SPAM, chopped fine

1 TB. butter

2 Granny Smith apples, peeled, cored, and chopped

1 shallot, minced fine

1 small tomato, seeded and diced

2 tsp. apple cider vinegar

½ cup apple cider

2 tsp. Dijon mustard

4 cups pork stock, reduced by ½

1 Vidalia onion, caramelized, peeled, and diced

3 TB. sage

3 oz. SPAM Lite, sautéed and finely chopped

1 large Washington apple

1. Add to a 6-inch bamboo skewer in order: 1 green bell pepper piece, 1 pineapple chunk, 1 SPAM medallion, 1 pineapple chunk, 1 SPAM medallion, 1 pineapple chunk, and 1 green bell pepper piece. Make 2 and set both aside.

2. Mix corn kernels with chorizo pieces, tricolored bell peppers, and Smoked SPAM. Sauté mixture about 5 minutes or until hot and spices are thoroughly mixed. Set aside and keep warm.

3. Melt butter in a saucepan over medium heat. Add Granny Smith apples and brown. Add shallots and tomato and cook for several minutes. Add vinegar and cider and reduce until almost dry. Add Dijon mustard and reduced pork stock. Finish by adding onion, sage, and SPAM Lite.

4. To serve, brush a little sauce on kebobs and grill 5 to 7 minutes or until SPAM is thoroughly heated.

5. Cut a 1-inch hole through the middle of Washington apple at a right angle to the core and set in the 12 o'clock position. Put the 2 kebobs into apple hole and separate so the ends of the skewers are at the 7 and 5 o'clock positions. Spoon the rest of sauce over kebobs and garnish with fresh herbs.

Herb-Crusted Rack of SPAM

Adapted from the recipe by David Spooner

---

2 TB. fresh rosemary leaves, minced	1 tsp. nutmeg
2 TB. fresh sage leaves, minced	Pinch salt and pepper
2 TB. fresh parsley leaves, minced	2 cups grits, cooked
2 TB. fresh thyme leaves, minced	Flour as needed
2 (12-oz.) cans SPAM luncheon meat	Butter as needed
3 bones from French-cut lamb chops, cooked and cleaned	¼ cup blue cheese
	2 cups port wine
2 butternut squash	1 leek, blanched, with green part cut into a long string
1 (12-oz.) can SPAM Lite	
2 cups butter	Fresh herb bouquet
2 tsp. cinnamon	

---

1. Combine rosemary, sage, parsley, and thyme in a small bowl. Set aside.

2. Cut 1 can SPAM into 3 parts and insert a lamb bone into each piece to form the "chop." Trim excess SPAM to create the shape of a lamb chop; they should look like a French-cut lamb chop with a clean bone sticking 3 to 4 inches out of the top of SPAM.

3. Rub each "chop" with herb mixture and grill on medium-high heat until desired degree of doneness, turning the chops halfway through the cooking. Set aside and keep warm.

4. Peel, clean, and cut squash into 1-inch cubes. Add squash to boiling water and cook until tender. Drain and set aside.

5. Cut ½ can SPAM Lite into 1-inch cubes and add to a food processor along with cooked squash, butter, cinnamon, nutmeg, salt, and pepper. Purée until smooth. (If mixture is too watery, add it to a sauté pan and cook until dry and the consistency of mashed potatoes.)

6. Spread cooked grits ½-inch thick on standard cookie sheet pan and let cool. Cut grits with a pig-shaped cookie cutter. Dust each "pig" with flour, and pan-fry until golden brown and crispy on each side, adding more butter for each batch as needed.

7. Thinly slice remaining 1 can SPAM and heat until warm and flexible. Put 1 tablespoon blue cheese on the end of each SPAM slice and roll up, holding each piece with a small toothpick to prevent SPAMGETTA from unrolling.

8. Pour wine into a small saucepan and bring to a boil over high heat. Reduce the heat to a simmer, and continue cooking until wine is reduced to about ¼ cup. Remove from heat, and let cool.

9. Put squash mixture in center of a plate and form into a mound about 4 inches high. Stand 3 SPAM chops, with bone part of chop toward squash, around the mound using squash to hold chops up, crossing bones like a teepee, and tying bones together with leek string. Arrange several crispy grits and several SPAMGETTA rolls around plate, and drizzle port wine reduction over SPAMGETTA rolls. Garnish with fresh herbs and serve.

SPAMRANGOONS

Adapted from the recipe by Paul Germarath, Scott Zublin, and Richardo Cabeza

---

2 (12-oz.) cans SPAM luncheon meat

1 (8-oz.) pkg. cream cheese

6 medium onions

1 tsp. chopped ginger (secret ingredient)

¼ cup fresh parsley, chopped

1 TB. black pepper

1 TB. Louisiana hot sauce

1 TB. Worcestershire sauce

2 qt. peanut oil

1 pkg. wonton wrappers

Salt

---

1. In the bowl of a food processor, mix SPAM, cream cheese, onions, ginger, parsley, black pepper, hot sauce, and Worcestershire sauce.

2. Heat peanut oil in a deep fryer or large pot to 375°F.

3. Lay out wanton wrappers one at a time, and moisten edges with water. Dab approximately 1 teaspoon SPAM mixture in the center of each wrapper. Fold wrapper around SPAM any way you like, making sure to have a good seal. (Wetting the edges helps provide this good seal.)

4. Fry wontons for several minutes or until they're golden brown and floating in the oil. Remove wontons from oil, salt lightly, and serve hot.

SPAM Oscar

Adapted from the recipe by John Meyers

2 eggs	2 cups Italian breadcrumbs
Dash salt and pepper	2 TB. butter
Dash Tabasco sauce	8 blanched asparagus spears
1 (12-oz.) can SPAM luncheon meat	2 oz. crabmeat
1 cup flour	2 cups Sauce Béarnaise (recipe follows)

1. In a shallow bowl, mix eggs, salt, pepper, and Tabasco sauce.

2. Slice SPAM longways to make medallions. Dredge medallions in order in flour, egg wash, and Italian breadcrumbs.

3. In a sauté pan over medium heat, melt butter. Sauté coated SPAM medallions in sizzling butter for 3 or 4 minutes or until golden brown on both sides. Pat SPAM with paper towels to remove excess butter.

4. Place two medallions on a plate. Cross 2 asparagus spears over SPAM, and place fresh crabmeat in asparagus cross. Ladle Sauce Béarnaise over the center of the dish, and serve. This is perfect paired with oven-browned new potatoes and caramelized carrot spears.

Sauce Béarnaise

6 sprigs fresh or 4 sprigs bottled tarragon (with 2 TB. liquid from bottle)	2 heaping TB. finely chopped cilantro leaves
⅓ cup tarragon vinegar (plus 2 more TB. if using fresh tarragon)	4 egg yolks
⅓ cup dry white wine	1 TB. heavy cream
4 garlic cloves	Pinch salt
1 heaping TB. very finely chopped shallots	Dash cayenne
	½ lb. clarified butter

1. Reserve leaves from ½ of tarragon stalks and set aside.

2. In a small heavy saucepan, combine vinegar, wine, garlic, shallots, and tarragon with liquid. Cook over high heat until liquid is reduced to ⅓ cup or less.

3. Strain through a fine sieve. Add cilantro and remaining tarragon, stir, and set Tarragon Reduction aside.

4. In a stainless-steel bowl, blend eggs, cream, salt, and cayenne. Set the bowl over boiling water, and stir constantly until mixture is very creamy. *Do not overcook.* Remove bowl from heat and continue to whisk until warm.

5. Add clarified butter a little at a time, whisking constantly. It's very important that butter is warm, not hot. When all butter is incorporated, add Tarragon Reduction very slowly. If sauce breaks, cook 1 egg yolk until creamy and whisk in broken sauce a little at a time.

INTERNATIONAL HORSERADISH FESTIVAL

Collinsville, Illinois
June
Dawn Cordle (dcordle@yourjournal.com)
www.horseradishfestival.com

The International Horseradish Festival in Collinsville, Illinois—the Horseradish Capital of the World—has been celebrating the versatile and greatly underutilized spicy member of the mustard family for more than 17 years.

Uniting people from around Collinsville as well as the Midwest, the International Horseradish Festival welcomes fun, entertainment, and great food and drink. Proceeds from the festival continue to aid local organizations, along with helping build playgrounds, assisting disabled children, and purchasing sporting equipment for local teams. The International Horseradish Festival is perhaps best known for its contests. Each year, eager contestants compete to see who can make the best Bloody Mary along with the best recipe featuring horseradish. Other events include a Little Miss Horseradish beauty pageant and an Annual Root Derby.

Speaking of root, the horseradish root is often harvested in the Spring and Fall when it's sold in 1,200-pound pallets to processors who grate the root, releasing the volatile oils that distinguish horseradish from all other flavors. The ground horseradish is then mixed with distilled vinegar to stabilize the "heat." This straightforward method varies from processor to processor. In the United States alone, an estimated 24 million pounds of horseradish roots are ground and processed annually to produce approximately 6 million gallons of prepared horseradish every year.

To savor horseradish at its best, buy only the amount you can use in a reasonable time. Keep in a tightly covered jar in the refrigerator to retain freshness. And always serve the desired amount of horseradish in a glass or ceramic bowl (it tarnishes silver), returning the tightly closed jar to the refrigerator immediately. Horseradish that remains unrefrigerated will gradually lose its flavor.

(International Horseradish Festival)

Carrot Horseradish Casserole

Adapted from the recipe by Mary Beth Heberer

4½ cups sliced carrots, uncooked	¼ tsp. salt
½ cup salad dressing (Miracle Whip)	Dash pepper
2 TB. onion, chopped	½ cup seasoned breadcrumbs
2 TB. prepared horseradish	2 TB. butter, melted

1. Preheat the oven to 350°F.

2. Cook carrots in boiling salted water for 10 minutes or until tender. Drain.

3. Combine salad dressing, onion, horseradish, salt, and pepper in a mixing bowl. Combine with carrots and place in a 1-quart casserole dish.

4. Mix breadcrumbs and melted butter, and sprinkle over carrots.

5. Bake, uncovered, for 30 minutes.

Horseradish Potatoes

Adapted from the recipe by Doris Huwer

---

2 lb. potatoes, peeled and boiled

¼ cup butter

2 TB. all-purpose flour

½ tsp. prepared mustard

2 cups beef stock

2 large eggs, beaten

½ cup half-and-half

¾ cup prepared horseradish

1 tsp. salt

¼ tsp. pepper

Paprika

---

1. Preheat the oven to 350°F.

2. Place cooked potatoes in a 2-quart baking dish.

3. Melt butter in a double boiler. Gradually stir in flour and mustard. Add stock and stir. Cook over medium heat until mixture thickens.

4. Beat together eggs and half-and-half. Add to mixture in the double boiler, and cook until thick. Add horseradish and salt and pepper to taste. If horseradish is hot, you might not need salt and pepper.

5. Pour sauce over cooked potatoes in the baking dish. Sprinkle with paprika, and bake for 15 to 20 minutes or until slightly brown.

Midwest Gourmet Chicken and Horsy Sauce

Adapted from the recipe by Linda Clenney

---

6 boneless, skinless chicken breast halves

Pepper

1 (10-oz.) box frozen chopped spinach, thawed

4 oz. farmer cheese, shredded

¼ cup plus 3 TB. prepared horseradish

12 strips country-style bacon

2 TB. margarine

1 TB. cornstarch

1 cup skim milk

1 tsp. dry mustard

2½ TB. granulated sugar

3 TB. vinegar

½ tsp. hot pepper sauce

½ tsp. black and red pepper or to taste

---

1. Preheat the oven to 325°F.

2. Pound chicken breasts just to thin out the thicker parts, and season with pepper.

3. Drain liquid from thawed spinach; do not cook. Combine spinach with cheese and ¼ cup horseradish, and spread mixture onto chicken breasts. (Spinach mixture may not totally cover chicken; that's okay.)

4. Roll up chicken breasts, wrap 2 pieces of bacon around each chicken breast, and secure with toothpicks. Place chicken rolls on a baking rack in a baking dish. Bake, uncovered, for 1 hour.

5. While chicken cooks, melt margarine in a saucepan over medium-high heat. Stir in cornstarch until dissolved, and stir in milk. Bring to a boil, stirring constantly. Reduce heat and boil for 1 minute.

6. Remove the pan from heat, and stir in remaining 3 tablespoons horseradish, mustard, sugar, vinegar, hot pepper sauce, and ½ teaspoon black and red pepper. Serve warm Horsy Sauce on the side with chicken.

Part 2

Main Dishes

MEAT AND POULTRY

FORT HARROD BEEF FESTIVAL

Harrodsburg, Kentucky
June
209-644-3755
www.fortharrodbeeffestival.org

Welcome to Harrodsburg, Kentucky, and the annual Fort Harrod Beef Festival. For those looking for a fun, exciting, and educational weekend packed with activities, this newly formed festival is the place to be.

The Fort Harrod Beef Festival was quickly formed to help promote and educate the rest of America about the production, distribution, and selling of beef from the farm to the marketplace. The popular event is loaded with concerts headlining local musicians and singers, arts and crafts, a vintage car show, a 5K race, and plenty of children's activities. The main attraction people come for, of course, is the Kentucky beef.

Visitors receive a beef education as they pull up a chair at the festival's steak and egg breakfast, attend the beef and bourbon tasting, sample the festival foods featuring Kentucky's finest cattle, and cheer on participants at the highly competitive beef and brisket grill-offs. Here, backyard barbecuers and professional chefs come together to find out who can grill the best steak or hamburger in town.

Today, many of the farmers in Kentucky have chosen to move away from raising tobacco—once the popular cash crop in the Bluegrass State—and are now raising beef cattle, proven by Kentucky having the largest inventory of beef cattle this side of the Mississippi.

The Fort Harrod Beef Festival, along with the Kentucky Beef Council, encourages people to include beef as part of their everyday diet. Beef is an excellent source of protein, the building block for muscles that aid metabolism. Beef is an excellent source of zinc, which helps fight colds and boosts the immune system. For children, beef is a good source of iron, vital to a child's mental development. And beef provides a healthy source of B vitamins, which aid in turning food into energy. These are just some of the facts you'll learn while attending the Fort Harrod Beef Festival in Harrodsburg, Kentucky.

(James O. Fraioli)

High Mountain Beef Brisket

Adapted from the recipe by Thomas C. Brown
and Dunn's Barbeque of Harrodsburg

---

1 (8-lb.) fatted brisket	Garlic powder
½ cup lemon juice	Black pepper
1 can high-quality beer	Seasoning salt

---

1. Place brisket in an aluminum tray with fat layer on top. Be sure to roll brisket so the small flap is tucked under. Pour lemon juice and beer over the top of brisket. Season meat generously with garlic powder and pepper and lightly with seasoning salt.

2. Load a 25- to 50-gallon smoker or outdoor grill with ½ bag of charcoal (with mesquite wood chips for flavor), all on one side, and light the coals. When the coals are gray and ashed over, place brisket on the opposite side of the smoker and cook indirectly (with no coals underneath meat).

3. Close the lid and cook for 5 to 7 hours. Meat should be very soft to the touch. Add more charcoal and cook for an additional 3 hours if meat isn't done. Remove, cool brisket, and slice.

Sweet Dunn Brisket

Adapted from the recipe by Thomas C. Brown
and Dunn's Barbeque of Harrodsburg

---

1 sweet onion	Garlic cloves, crushed
1 (10- to 12-lb.) brisket, untrimmed	Dry mustard
1 bunch rosemary	Steak seasoning salt

---

1. The day before, rub sweet onion in butter, roll in sugar to coat, wrap in aluminum foil, and let sit at room temperature for at least 24 hours.

2. Preheat the oven to 325°F.

3. Spice brisket heavily on both sides with rosemary, garlic, and dry mustard and lightly with seasoning salt. Wrap brisket in aluminum foil, and place in a cooking pan. Cook for about 3 hours.

4. Remove foil wrapper and place brisket back in the pan.

5. Remove foil from onion and cut onion in slices. Lay onion slices on top of brisket. Cover the pan, and cook for another 3 hours or until internal temperature reaches 175°F.

6. Remove brisket from the oven, trim, and slice while warm.

Steak Dunn Up

Adapted from the recipe by Thomas C. Brown
and Dunn's Barbeque of Harrodsburg

---

4 premium thick, hand-cut steaks (rib eye, New York, filet mignon)

Steak seasoning salt

Garlic cloves, crushed

Black pepper

1 onion, sliced and grilled

High-quality blue cheese dressing

---

1. Heat the grill to high heat.

2. Season steak with seasoning salt, garlic, and black pepper. Grill until internal temperature is 145°F for medium-rare or continue to grill until desired doneness.

3. Plate steaks and top with grilled onion slices and a dash of blue cheese dressing.

Backyard Burger

Adapted from the recipe by Thomas C. Brown
and Dunn's Barbeque of Harrodsburg

Yield: 4 servings

---

1 (1.1-oz.) pkg. Lipton's Onion or Mushroom Onion dip mix

2 lb. lean ground beef

Steak seasoning salt

Black pepper

Garlic cloves, crushed

---

1. Mix onion dip mix with ground beef. Season lightly with seasoning salt, pepper, and garlic.

2. Form mixture into burgers and grill until burgers are desired texture and taste.

Sassafras Filet Mignon

Adapted from the recipe by Thomas C. Brown
and Dunn's Barbeque of Harrodsburg

Yield: 4 to 6 servings

1 beef loin	Coarsely ground black pepper
Fresh lemon juice	Steak seasoning salt
Garlic powder	Small piece sassafras

1. Preheat a smoker to 300°F to 350°F.

2. Cut steaks 2 inches thick from loin. Place steaks side by side and close together in an outdoor smoker, not directly over the fire, but at least 10 inches away from the coals, indirectly.

3. Baste steaks with lemon juice, and season with garlic powder, black pepper, and seasoning salt. Close the smoker and run for 20 minutes.

4. After 20 minutes, place sassafras on the coals and smoke for an additional 15 minutes.

5. If desired, place steaks directly over the coals for 30 to 40 seconds to mark meat before serving.

NATIONAL BARBECUE FESTIVAL

Douglas, Georgia
November
1-800-385-0002
www.nationalbbqfestival.com

The National Barbecue Festival in Douglas, Georgia, is one of the largest attended barbecue events in America. More than 50,000 visitors from around the country come to watch the "Best of the Best" barbecue teams compete against one another. Fifty thousand dollars in cash and prizes are awarded each year, as a panel of veteran judges sample and score the best barbecue dishes. Think you have what it takes? If so, the National BBQ Festival is the place to be.

About 13 barbecue sanctioning networks exist across the United States. To be considered one of America's "best" grillers, the National BBQ Festival invites the top five-point champions in each sanctioning group to the annual "Best of the Best" Cook-Off competition. During the highly anticipated cook-offs, the celebrated barbecue teams square off by grilling their secret recipes for chicken, ribs, pork, pork chops, brisket, and whole hog. In addition to the international event, there's also the Open, Backyard, Kid's Q Apple and Sweet Potato Pie, and People's Choice events held the following day.

Attendees to the 2-day festival are in for a real treat, as there's enough barbecue for everyone—well, almost. At last year's festival, five large barbecue vendors sold out of barbecue by day's end. In fact, everything from a $17,000 barbecue to a pulled pork sandwich was purchased.

The popular barbecue festival, which has been featured on the Food Network and PBS, kicks off annually with an opening ceremony followed by the Parade of Teams. The barbecue competitions commence throughout the bustling event, as guests applaud their favorite grillers while dining on some of the best barbecue in America. Entertainment includes live musicians and art shows hosted by local and area artisans. There's also South Georgia's Largest Indoor Yard Sale, where more than 7,000 visitors search for that lifetime treasure.

(National BBQ Festival)

Big Bob Gibson BBQ Championship Pork Shoulder

Adapted from the recipe by Chief Cook Chris Lilly

¾ cup apple juice	⅓ cup kosher salt
½ cup water	1 TB. chili powder
1 cup sugar	1 tsp. oregano leaves
¼ cup salt	1 tsp. cayenne
2 TB. Worcestershire sauce	1 tsp. ground cumin
1 (16-lb.) whole pork shoulder	1 tsp. black pepper
¼ cup dark brown sugar	1 (5-oz.) bottle Big Bob Gibson Championship Red Sauce (or your favorite)
½ cup paprika	
⅓ cup garlic salt	

1. In a bowl, combine apple juice, water, ½ cup sugar, salt, and Worcestershire sauce. Using a flavor injector, available at most kitchen and cookware stores, inject pork shoulder evenly with injection solution.

2. In a bowl, combine brown sugar, remaining ½ cup sugar, paprika, garlic salt, kosher salt, chili powder, oregano leaves, cayenne, cumin, and black pepper. Apply a generous amount of rub to meat, patting so rub adheres.

3. Preheat the smoker to 225°F.

4. Place shoulder in the smoker and cook with indirect heat for 16 hours. When done, pork should pull off bones easily and the internal temperature should reach 195°F.

5. Serve shoulder with sauce on the side or paint shoulder with sauce the last 20 minutes of cooking.

Southern Ribs

Adapted from the recipe by the National Barbecue Festival Committee

---

Yield: 4 to 6 servings

Salt and pepper

2 racks pork ribs, membrane removed

1 cup dark brown sugar

Cayenne

---

1. Preheat the smoker to 165°F.

2. Salt and pepper ribs and put them on an oiled grill rack in a smoker for 4 hours.

3. When cooked, remove ribs from the smoker, place on aluminum foil, and generously rub both sides with brown sugar. Sprinkle a small amount of cayenne on each side.

4. Completely seal ribs in a double thickness of heavy-duty aluminum foil, sealing each layer separately. Put ribs back in the smoker or on indirect heat for 1 or 2 hours.

5. Cut ribs apart and serve.

Grilled Vidalia Onion

Adapted from the recipe by the National Barbecue Festival Committee—
and an excellent side dish for BBQ

Yield: 8 servings

4 large Vidalia onions	4 tsp. your favorite BBQ rub
4 TB. butter or margarine	

1. Wash onions and peel the first layer of skin. Cut or scoop a hole in the top to accommodate 1 tablespoon butter or margarine and 1 teaspoon of your favorite barbecue rub.

2. Fill the opening with butter and rub, and place onions in a pouch of heavy-duty aluminum foil, leaving the top open to allow onion to absorb smoke and turn light brown.

3. Grill for 15 to 20 minutes over direct medium heat or until onions are soft. Cut onions in half, sprinkle with a little extra rub, and serve hot.

Grilled Banana Split

Adapted from the recipe by the National Barbecue Festival Committee

Yield: 8 servings

8 firm bananas	1 (16-oz.) bag miniature marshmallows
4 (3-oz.) chocolate bars, broken into squares	Chopped pecans
	8 scoops vanilla ice cream

1. Wash bananas and cut a slit into the top curve of banana, through the peel, being careful not to go all the way through the bottom peel.

2. Carefully pull each banana apart just enough to stuff with chocolate squares, marshmallows, and chopped pecans as best you can.

3. Wrap each banana in heavy-duty aluminum foil, place on the grill over direct medium heat, and cook for at least 30 minutes. Leave on the grill until ready to serve.

4. To serve, open the foil and make a boat. Banana skin should be dark and banana should be soft. Squeeze banana toward the middle from both ends, making a larger boat, and fill with a generous scoop of vanilla ice cream. Sprinkle with more pecans, and serve.

INTERNATIONAL CHILI SOCIETY WORLD CHAMPIONSHIP CHILI COOK-OFFS

Varying locations
October
877-777-4427
www.chilicookoff.com

From the time chili peppers were mixed with meat and cooked, the great chili debate was on. Today, it's more of a war to see who can brew up the best bowl of chili in the world. Over the past 150 years, many personalities and anecdotes have been linked with chili. It has been praised by presidents, defended by Hollywood celebrities, and it's said Will Rogers even judged a town by its chili.

Today, the International Chili Society (ICS) sees to it that every "heated" chili competition is correctly carried out. The ICS is a nonprofit organization that sanctions chili cook-offs with judging, cooking rules, and regulations. These cook-offs are held worldwide and benefit a long list of worthwhile charities. Many of the ICS-sanctioned cook-offs include cash prizes and awards at the World's Championship Chili Cook-Off (WCCC), held every year in October in various parts of the country. The WCCC is the largest food festival in the world, attracting millions of dollars and millions of chili aficionados who taste, cook, and judge more than 200 cook-offs.

The ICF-sanctioned cook-offs include three categories: Red (traditional red chili), Chili Verde (green chili), and Salsa. A World Champion is crowned in each category. To locate an official ICS Chili Cook-Off in your area, log on to the ICS website and choose a state from the map or list. To sort by date, simply search for a specific cook-off.

What does it take to be a World Chili Champion? The ICS won't give away all the secrets, but a good place to start is by reviewing the World Champion Chili Cooks and the recipes that earned them their titles over the years. You never know, you may be the next World Chili Champion!

(International Chili Society)

World Championship Gold Miner's Chili

Adapted from the recipe by Steve Falkowski

1½ cups white onion, finely minced

8 garlic cloves, finely minced

2 (15.5-oz.) cans chicken broth, with fat removed

½ (8-oz.) can Hunt's tomato sauce

¾ tsp. garlic powder

3 TB. ground cumin

10½ TB. chili powder, or 5 TB. California chili powder (mild) and 4½ TB. New Mexico chili powder (hot)

2 tsp. salt

3 lb. beef, cut into ¼-in. cubes

1 TB. Wesson oil

½ tsp. meat tenderizer

½ tsp. light brown sugar

1 tsp. Tabasco sauce

---

1. In a large pot over medium heat, simmer onion and garlic in 2 cups chicken broth for 10 minutes. Add tomato sauce, garlic powder, cumin, chili powder, and salt, and mix well.

2. In a separate pan over medium-high heat, brown meat in oil and drain well.

3. Sprinkle meat with tenderizer and add to onion-spice mixture. Add remaining broth and simmer for 2½ hours.

4. Mix in brown sugar and Tabasco sauce just before serving.

Kathouse Chili Verde

Adapted from the recipe by Kathy and Mike Stewart

2 onions, minced	1 lb. hot green chilies, chopped
3 cloves garlic, minced	1 lb. mild green chilies, chopped
4 lb. pork, cubed	1½ lb. tomatillos, chopped
Salt and pepper	1 tsp. dried oregano
4 TB. oil	2 jalapeños, minced
4 cups chicken broth	2 TB. cumin
2 bay leaves	¼ cup freshly chopped cilantro

1. Sauté onions and garlic in a large pot with 2 tablespoons oil over medium heat.

2. In a separate pan over medium-high heat, brown pork with salt and pepper in 2 tablespoons oil. Add onions and garlic. Add chicken broth, bay leaves, hot green chilies, mild green chilies, tomatillos, oregano, jalapeños, and cumin. Reduce to medium heat, cover, and simmer.

3. About ½ hour before cooking is completed, remove bay leaves and add chopped cilantro. Add salt to taste.

Gunny Mike's Devil Dog Chili

Adapted from the recipe by Mike Piserchia

4 (12-oz.) links hot Italian sausage, at room temperature

1 jalapeño pepper

1 habanero pepper

1 red chili pepper

2 TB. extra-virgin olive oil

2 lb. sirloin steak, at room temperature

½ cup flour

1 lb. ground beef (90 percent lean), at room temperature

1 large Vidalia onion, coarsely chopped

1 TB. garlic salt

2 tsp. cumin

1 tsp. dried basil

1 tsp. minced garlic

1 tsp. minced onion

1 tsp. salt

1 tsp. red pepper

¼ cup chili powder

1 tsp. dried oregano

1 tsp. paprika

1 TB. yellow cornmeal

2 (12-oz.) cans beef broth

1 (14.5-oz.) cans diced tomatoes, drained

2 (12-oz.) cans tomato paste

1 cup finely chopped fresh cilantro

3 large bay leaves

1 cinnamon stick

1 TB. Masa

¼ cup warm water

1. Remove casing from sausage, and cut sausage into ½-inch cubes. Set aside.

2. Slit jalapeño, habanero, and red chili peppers lengthwise 3 times. Set aside.

3. Add olive oil to a large, heavy, stainless-steel frying pan set over medium to high heat.

4. Cut steak into 1-inch cubes. Lightly coat with flour, add to the frying pan, and brown. Remove browned sirloin with a slotted spoon to an 8-quart stainless-steel pot.

5. Add ground beef, sausage, and Vidalia onion to the frying pan and brown, breaking up any lumps. Add mixture to the pot with sirloin.

6. Stir in garlic salt, cumin, basil, garlic, minced onion, salt, red pepper, chili powder, oregano, paprika, cornmeal, beef broth, diced tomatoes, tomato paste, cilantro, and bay leaves. Add cinnamon stick and peppers last. Bring to a boil, reduce heat to low, and simmer for 2 hours, stirring frequently.

7. In a small bowl, add Masa to warm water and stir until a thin paste forms. Add to the pot 15 minutes before the end of cooking, and stir.

8. Before serving, remove and discard cinnamon stick, bay leaves, and all peppers.

Two Teachers' Salsa

Adapted from the recipe by Stephen J. Moir and Jeffrey Bicsko,
New Jersey State Chili and Salsa Cook-Off

3 lb. Roma tomatoes, very ripe, diced	5 TB. fresh cilantro, chopped
2 tsp. salt	2 tsp. lime zest
1 green bell pepper, finely diced	Juice of 3 limes
1 red bell pepper, finely diced	Salt and pepper
1 large sweet onion, finely diced	Tabasco sauce
2 chipotle peppers in adobo, minced	

1. Place tomatoes in a large bowl and sprinkle with salt to allow natural juices to come out. Refrigerate for 30 minutes.

2. Add green bell pepper, red bell pepper, onion, and chipotle peppers, and mix well. Let rest overnight, refrigerated.

3. When ready to serve, add cilantro, lime zest, and lime juice, and mix thoroughly. Season with salt, pepper, and Tabasco sauce, and serve cold.

Chillie Willie's Chili-Salsa

Adapted from the recipe by Judith Omerza

Yield: 4 cups

1 medium Vidalia onion	1 pt. grape tomatoes
1 medium white onion	2 large tomatoes
2 large Anaheim peppers	1 small turnip
2 jalapeño peppers	Juice of 1 lime
2 habanero peppers	Juice of 1 lemon
1 large bunch fresh cilantro	Salt and cumin
1 pt. cherry tomatoes	

1. Chop Vidalia onion, white onion, Anaheim peppers, jalapeño peppers, habanero peppers, cilantro, cherry tomatoes, grape tomatoes, large tomatoes, and turnip. Add to a bowl.

2. Add lime juice, lemon juice, salt, and cumin. Chill until ready to serve.

GREAT AMERICAN HOT DOG FESTIVAL

Columbus, Ohio
July
email@hotdogfestival.com
www.hotdogfestival.com

Hot dog lovers around the country, mark your calendars for The Great American Hot Dog Festival! Held in Columbus, Ohio, every July (National Hot Dog Month) and home to the "World's Longest Hot Dog," The Great American Hot Dog Festival invites visitors from near and far to join in some serious fun and celebration. The festival begins a pre-event campaign led by a dedicated team of Hotdoggers who hit the streets passing out fliers and other promotional items to get the word out about the festival. And there's a lot to promote!

Feeling adventurous? Enter the hot dog eating contest to see if you can devour the most hot dogs in a short amount of time. Have a favorite hot dog recipe? Now's your chance to participate in the popular Hot Dog Cook-Off. The winning recipes are published locally in an annual *Fire House Hot! Hot! Hot! Hot Dog Cookbook*.

For those who may not have a winning hot dog recipe, perhaps there's a winning dog. That's right, the hot dog festival includes a Pretty Pooch Contest. If your four-legged friend can sing, dance, jump, or dress to impress, your pet has a good chance of winning. There's also a Pie Throwing Contest, a Hot Dog Idol—Karaoke Contest, and an Elvis Impersonator Contest. Who says you have to travel to Las Vegas to see one of these?

Other than the extravagant contests, there's plenty of noncompetitive activities for the entire family. The Great American Hot Dog Festival offers carnival rides, a classic car show, live music, face painting, and plenty of food vendors selling non–hot dog treats like funnel cakes and snow cones.

(Great American Hot Dog Festival)

Kitty's Hot Dog Coney Sauce

Adapted from the recipe by Kitty Coyne

Yield: 4 to 6 servings

1 lb. lean ground beef	2 TB. ketchup
½ tsp. salt	2 TB. chili powder
⅛ tsp. ground black pepper	Water
1 TB. paprika	

1. In a large skillet over medium-high heat, brown ground beef for 3 to 5 minutes. Drain.

2. Stir in salt, pepper, paprika, ketchup, and chili powder. Add water to cover, and simmer until water is absorbed, stirring frequently, 10 to 15 minutes.

3. Spoon sauce over the best all-beef hot dogs you can find, but not before adding a dab of mustard. (Never put ketchup on a hot dog!) Serve sprinkled with chopped, white onions.

Kitty's Southern Slaw

Adapted from the recipe by Kitty Coyne

Yield: 4 to 6 servings

1 cup ranch dressing	1 tsp. celery seed
1 cup Miracle Whip or mayonnaise	½ TB. freshly ground black pepper
3 TB. cider vinegar	6 cups shredded cabbage (purple and green)
2 TB. granulated sugar	1 cup shredded carrots

1. In a medium bowl, combine ranch dressing, Miracle Whip, vinegar, sugar, celery seed, and pepper.

2. In a large bowl, combine cabbage and carrots. Pour dressing mixture over cabbage mixture, and toss gently to coat. Cover and refrigerate overnight or until serving time, at least 2 hours.

Uncle Al's T-N-T Chili

Adapted from the recipe by Albert Coyne

Yield: 6 to 8 servings

2 lb. ground beef	1½ cups water
2 medium onions, chopped	6 or 7 jalapeño peppers, rinsed and chopped
1 medium green bell pepper, seeds and ribs removed, and chopped	
1 stalk celery	¼ cup chili powder
1 clove garlic, minced	½ tsp. salt
2 (16-oz.) cans tomatoes, chopped	1 TB. ground red pepper
1 (15-oz.) can tomato sauce	½ tsp. pepper
	1 bay leaf

1. In a pan over medium heat, brown ground beef, onions, bell pepper, celery, and garlic.

2. Add tomatoes, tomato sauce, water, jalapeño peppers, chili powder, salt, ground red pepper, pepper, and bay leaf. Simmer and stir until hot. Remove bay leaf before serving.

NATIONAL HAMBURGER FESTIVAL

Akron, Ohio
August
716-565-4141
www.hamburgerfestival.com

The city of Akron, Ohio, is home to the ever-popular hamburger. The Menches family has long laid claim to being the original creators of the sandwich. According to the Menches, their ancestors, Frank and Charles Menches, two brothers who lived and worked in Akron, invented the hamburger at the New York State Fair in 1885. To support Akron's legendary inventors, Akron recently launched the first-ever National Hamburger Festival, attracting hamburger connoisseurs from around the country to take part in food, music, and fun.

Meanwhile, in Seymour, Wisconsin, residents believe their local son Charlie Nagreen invented the sandwich. New Haven, Connecticut, insists it's Louis Lasser who flipped the first burger in 1900. Or was it Fletcher Davis of Athens, Texas, who did it first, in 1904?

Regardless of who invented the tasty sandwich, the National Hamburger Festival is the creation of Drew Cerza, president and CEO of the RMI Promotion Group of New York, which also invented the highly successful National Buffalo Wing Festival in Buffalo, New York. According to Cerza, Akron is the perfect place for a great national festival because Akron is an all-American city and home to the National Inventor's Hall of Fame and the National Football Hall of Fame. Akron is now being branded the "Hamburger Capital of the World."

Thousands of visitors who travel to the National Hamburger Festival are greeted with more than 15 local and national restaurants serving their hamburger specialties. More than 40 different styles of burgers are served in sample sizes with additional summer fare and Akron's favorite foods. The festival also offers live music, children's activities, and contests galore, including a Bobbing for Burgers contest, the Miss Hamburger Festival contest, and the Big Boy Ohio Hamburger Eating Championship, along with a Best Burger challenge for both amateurs and competing restaurants.

(National Hamburger Festival)

"Jack It Up" Burger

Adapted from the recipe by the National Hamburger Festival

Yield: 6 to 8 servings

2 lb. fresh ground round	1 clove garlic, minced
½ Vidalia onion, minced	Salt and pepper
1 egg white	1 cup sliced mushrooms
1 cup Jack Daniel's whiskey	½ Vidalia onion, sliced
1 TB. Worcestershire sauce	1 TB. butter
1 TB. molasses	6 to 8 kaiser rolls
1 TB. A.1. Steak Sauce	

1. In a bowl, mix together ground beef, minced onion, egg white, whiskey, Worcestershire sauce, molasses, steak sauce, and garlic. Season with salt and pepper. Shape mixture into 6 to 8 patties, and grill until done to your liking.

2. Meanwhile, place mushrooms and onion slices on a piece of aluminum foil, dot with butter, and fold foil to seal. Grill until mushrooms and onions are tender.

3. When meat is done, grill buns, cut sides down, until light brown.

4. Serve burgers on toasted buns, topped with mushrooms and onions.

Acropolis Burger on the Ranch

Adapted from the recipe by the National Hamburger Festival

Yield: 4 servings

1 lb. ground lamb	2 TB. minced fresh green onions
½ tsp. minced fresh basil	½ tsp. garlic powder
1 TB. fresh lemon juice	½ tsp. ground black pepper
2 cloves garlic, minced	½ tsp. celery seed
Dash salt and pepper	½ cup low-fat mayonnaise
3 hard rolls	Crumbled feta cheese
¼ cup powdered buttermilk	Sliced cucumber
½ cup milk	Sliced tomatoes
2 TB. minced Vidalia onion	Thick-sliced red onion

1. In a large bowl, mix lamb, basil, lemon juice, garlic, salt, and pepper. Shape mixture into 4 patties slightly larger than buns but no more than 1½ inches thick. Grill over medium-hot coals until no longer pink, or to your liking.

2. When meat is done, grill buns, cut sides down, until light brown. Place a burger on the bottom of each bun.

3. In a bowl, combine powdered buttermilk, milk, Vidalia onion, green onions, garlic powder, black pepper, celery seed, and mayonnaise. Cover and chill ranch dressing until ready to use.

4. Sprinkle burgers with feta cheese and top with cucumber, tomato, and onion slices. Pour a generous amount of ranch dressing on the cut side of top ½ of buns and over burgers before serving.

Max Burger

Adapted from the recipe by the National Hamburger Festival

Yield: 8 servings

1 lb. ground sirloin	1 TB. hot pepper sauce
10 minced fresh whole jalapeño peppers, including seeds	½ tsp. garlic salt
1 medium yellow onion, chopped	1 TB. white vinegar
1 (1-oz.) pkg. dry taco seasoning (hot)	8 potato buns

1. In a large bowl, combine sirloin, jalapeño peppers, onion, dry taco seasoning, hot pepper sauce, garlic salt, and white vinegar. Shape mixture into 8 patties, and grill over medium-hot coals until done.

2. When meat is done, grill buns, cut sides down, until light brown. Place a burger on the bottom of each bun.

Middle Eastern Kefte Burger

Adapted from the recipe by the National Hamburger Festival

Yield: 12 servings

1 lb. ground round	6 to 8 pita breads, cut in ½
1 cup fresh minced parsley	Thick plain yogurt or sour cream
6 green onions, chopped	2 cups minced tomatoes
½ cup freshly crushed mint leaves	Romaine leaves
1 TB. olive oil	1¼ cups crumbled feta cheese
2 TB. garlic powder	

1. In a bowl, combine ground round, parsley, green onions, mint, olive oil, and garlic powder. Shape mixture into 12 or more patties, and grill over medium-hot coals to desired degree of doneness.

2. Place burgers in pita pockets with yogurt, tomatoes, romaine leaves, and crumbled feta.

Chicken Fajita Burger

Adapted from the recipe by the National Hamburger Festival

Yield: 4 servings

2 lb. ground chicken (95 percent lean)	Olive oil
2 TB. chipotle chili powder	4 large sourdough hamburger buns
3 TB. chopped fresh cilantro	1½ cups shredded cheddar cheese
Several drops Tabasco sauce	Taco sauce
3 TB. your favorite grill seasoning powder	7 green onions, chopped
	Shredded lettuce

1. In a large bowl, mix chicken, chili powder, cilantro, Tabasco sauce, and grill seasoning. Shape mixture into 4 patties, drizzle olive oil over patties, and grill over medium-hot coals for 7 minutes per side or until meat is firm.

2. When meat is done, grill buns, cut side down, until light brown. Place burgers on buns.

3. Top with shredded cheese, taco sauce, green onions, and shredded lettuce.

NATIONAL BUFFALO WING FESTIVAL

Buffalo, New York
September
716-565-4141
www.buffalowing.com

Not only is Buffalo, New York, the third cleanest city in the United States, according to *Reader's Digest*, it's also the birthplace of what has become the most popular finger food in America—the buffalo wing. Buffalo wings are chicken wing sections that are deep-fried and coated in a spicy sauce. Although many variations of the sauce exist, the most common sauces combine cayenne pepper sauce, white vinegar, butter, salt, and garlic.

In 2002, a festival was created in the buffalo wing's honor. Today, festival founder Drew Cerza—who also founded the National Hamburger Festival—believes his National Buffalo Wing Festival is so popular that it will pave the way for the newly announced Chicken Wing Hall of Fame, further solidifying Buffalo as the Buffalo Wing Capital of the World.

Held every September in downtown Buffalo, the National Buffalo Wing Festival attracts thousands of die-hard buffalo wing fanatics who come to celebrate the buffalo-style chicken wing and the International Federation of Competitive Eating (IFOCE)–sanctioned buffalo wing eating contest. The festival also lures CNN, *Today*, the Travel Channel, the Food Network, the Discovery Channel, and various newspapers and magazines throughout the world.

Since the first National Buffalo Wing Festival was held, more than 1 million chicken wings have been consumed. But how many chicken wings can one individual eat in one sitting? Just ask Sonya Thomas, who entered the National Buffalo Wing Festival's Eating Contest in 2004. She consumed 161 chicken wings (that's over 5 pounds!) in 12 minutes. Her record has yet to be broken.

(National Buffalo Wing Festival)

Original Buffalo Chicken Wings

Adapted from the recipe by the National Buffalo Wing Festival

Yield: 6 to 8 appetizer servings

2½ lb. chicken wing pieces	⅓ cup melted butter
½ cup cayenne sauce	

1. Bake wings 1 hour at 425°F or deep-fry for 12 minutes at 400°F. To deep-fry, heat 4 cups vegetable oil over high heat in a deep skillet, Dutch oven, or deep-fat fryer until it sizzles (400°F). Add chicken wings in small batches and cook until they're golden and crisp, stirring occasionally. When done, remove wings to drain on paper towels and cook remaining wings.

2. Combine cayenne sauce and butter in a medium bowl, and keep warm. Dip wings in sauce to coat.

3. Serve wings with celery sticks and ranch dressing.

Chef Armand's Honey Dijon Chicken Wings

Adapted from the recipe by the National Buffalo Wing Festival

Yield: 6 to 8 appetizer servings

2½ lb. chicken wings, split, and tips discarded

½ cup honey

⅓ cup cayenne sauce

⅓ cup French's Napa Valley Style Dijon mustard

4 cups vegetable oil

1. Heat oil over high heat in a deep skillet, Dutch oven, or deep-fat fryer until it sizzles (400°F). Add chicken wings in small batches and cook until they're golden and crisp, stirring occasionally. When done, remove wings to drain on paper towels and cook remaining wings. Or bake wings in a single layer on a rack in a foil-lined roasting pan for 1 hour at 425°F until crisp and no longer pink, turning halfway through baking time. Or grill over a medium heat for 20 to 25 minutes. Drain thoroughly.

2. Combine honey, cayenne sauce, and mustard in medium bowl. Toss wings in sauce to coat.

Key Lime Mousse Chicken Wings

Adapted from the recipe by the National Buffalo Wing Festival

1 (.25-oz.) pkg. unflavored gelatin	1 TB. lime zest
3 TB. warm water	¼ tsp. vanilla extract
4 large eggs, separated, at room temperature	1 cup chilled whipping cream
	Shallots, chopped
⅔ cup fresh squeezed Key lime juice (16 to 20 Key limes)	Butter
¾ cup sugar	Habanero pepper
	Dry white wine

1. Sprinkle gelatin over warm water in a small bowl. Set aside to soften.

2. Whisk yolks in a small saucepan to blend. Whisk in lime juice, ½ cup sugar, and lime zest. Cook over low heat, stirring constantly, until mixture thickens to the consistency of heavy cream.

3. Remove the pan from heat, and stir in gelatin and vanilla extract. Set pan in cold water and cool to room temperature, stirring occasionally.

4. In a bowl, beat egg whites until soft peaks form.

5. In another large bowl, beat whipping cream until soft peaks form, add remaining ¼ cup sugar, and beat until stiff.

6. Fold egg whites into whipped cream.

7. In ⅓ increments, fold lime mixture into egg whites and cream. You can either divide mixture into 6 individual serving dishes or leave in the large bowl. Chill until set.

8. While mousse is chilling, make sauce. Sauté chopped shallots in butter until soft. Add habanero pepper a little at a time until desired heat is achieved. Add remaining lime juice and white wine. Reduce until thick.

9. To serve, spread a thin layer of mousse on a plate or platter, and place sauce-soaked wings on top.

Buffalo Barb
Championship Wing Sauce

Adapted from the recipe by the National Buffalo Wing Festival

Yield: 30 wings

30 medium-size chicken wings

1 oz. Wishbone Italian dressing

5 medium cloves garlic, crushed

3 dashes Worcestershire sauce

¾ cup butter

1½ cups hot sauce (plus Tabasco to your liking if you want really hot wings)

1 cup fresh grated Parmesan cheese

2 fresh lemons

1. Deep-fry chicken wings until crispy. Remove from fryer and place wings in a large bowl.

2. Heat a small saucepan over medium heat and add Italian dressing. Add garlic, sauté, and mix in Worcestershire sauce. Add butter and stir until completely melted. Add hot sauce and mix well until heated. Add Parmesan cheese and stir until completely melted.

3. Quarter lemons and squeeze juice onto cooked wings. Pour sauce over wings in the bowl, and toss until wings are completely covered with sauce.

4. Serve wings with carrots, celery, and blue cheese dressing.

The Big Dog's Very Hot Sauce

Adapted from the recipe by the National Buffalo Wing Festival

---

1 (23-oz.) bottle Frank's Red Hot Sauce

1 (12-oz.) bottle Louisiana Brand Hot Sauce

2 cups salted butter

¼ cup ketchup

¼ tsp. finely ground black pepper

½ clove fresh garlic, minced

½ cup Formerly Secret Aged 40 Hot Pepper Sauce (recipe follows)

---

1. In a large pot over medium-high heat, combine Frank's Red Hot Sauce, Louisiana Brand Hot Sauce, butter, ketchup, black pepper, and garlic.

2. When butter is melted, reduce heat to medium low and simmer for 1 hour, whisking thoroughly every 5 to 10 minutes.

3. Add Formerly Secret Aged 40 Hot Pepper Sauce. Stir and continue to simmer.

4. Use this sauce to coat fried chicken wings before serving.

Note: A traditional buffalo wing sauce is like a fingerprint—many sauce recipes exist, and every one is a little different. This sauce is for advanced wing eaters only. It's a traditional cayenne/butter-based sauce, but it adds a dizzying array of complexities in flavor, aroma, and heat from aged hot peppers along with a true intensity from the reduction process. This wing sauce isn't just tasted and smelled; it's truly experienced as new levels of taste, heat, aftertaste, and after-burn unfold over time. Enjoy … if you dare.

Formerly Secret Aged 40 Hot Pepper Sauce

---

4 lb. fresh hot peppers*

6 cups distilled white vinegar

1 TB. salt

1. Cut stems off peppers and add to a saucepan of boiling water. Boil over low heat for 3 minutes and then drain.

2. Combine peppers with vinegar and salt, and blend or process into liquid. (Do this in batches and mix together when done, if necessary.) Store in canning jars in the dark for up to 12 months.

*You can use any combination of chocolate habanero, habanero-red savina, Jamaican hot chocolate, Amazon, Antillais Caribbean, Aribibi gusano, Australian lantern, bazuka, billy goat, bird's eye, devil's tongue, aci sivri, Afghan, Aji omnicolor, Anaheim, ancho villa hybrid, Aurora, Bolivian rainbow, Chimayo, Chinese multi-color, datil, de arbol purple, false alarm hybrid, fatali, fire, five color, flame fountain, gold spike, Hawaiian red kona, Indonesian, jalapa hybrid, jalapeño jumbo, jalapeño purple, jaloro, kung pao hybrid, largo purple, limo, Tabasco, Tabasco greenleaf, or Thai red.

ALABAMA CHICKEN AND EGG FESTIVAL

Moulton, Alabama
April
256-974-1658
www.alabamachickenandeggfestival.com

The Alabama Chicken and Egg Festival, created to promote and educate the public on the economic impact and health values of poultry and eggs, is a 2-day outdoor extravaganza attracting more than 12,000 people annually. With plenty of food vendors, live entertainment, battle of the bands, an arts and crafts fair, children's activities, and an annual BBQ Chicken Cooking Contest, there's no shortage of fun and delicious poultry here.

Open to all barbecue connoisseurs in Alabama, the BBQ Chicken Cooking Contest is a fun and educational way to learn about the diverse grilling methods used in preparing and serving America's favorite bird. Contestants have the option of using charcoal or propane gas in their quest for barbecue stardom, which includes generous cash prizes and bragging rights for the year. Awards are also given to the Best Decorated Cook Site, based on setup, theme, creativity, and neatness.

Other popular activities at the Alabama Chicken and Egg Festival include a Chicken Clucking Contest, Chicken Wing Eating Contest, Hard Boiled Egg Eating Contest, Karaoke for Big Chickens, and the Alabama Farmers Agriculture Photography Contest.

According to the state of Alabama, agriculture is the number-one industry, which employs almost a half-million people—roughly 21 percent of the state's workforce. Producing more than 1 million chickens a year, Alabama is currently ranked as the third largest poultry producer in the nation.

While attending the festival, don't forget to check out the vast array of chicken- and egg-related items for sale, along with an Exotic Bantam Chicken Display where attendees have the opportunity to observe more than 100 chickens representing 25 different varieties.

(Alabama Chicken and Egg Festival)

Grilled Chicken and Pasta Salad

Adapted from the recipe by Della Miller

Yield: 8 servings

4 chicken breasts	2 (1-oz.) pkg. ranch dressing mix
2 TB. black pepper	1 TB. dried oregano
¼ cup steak sauce	2 TB. Italian seasoning
¼ cup water	2 cups tomatoes, diced
2 lb. macaroni, bowtie pasta, or spaghetti	2 cups cucumbers, diced
Olive oil	1 cup celery, diced
Salt	1 bunch green onions, diced
¼ cup vinegar	2 cups Italian salad dressing (light)
¼ cup sugar	2 cups shredded Colby and cheddar cheese
¼ cup water	6 TB. bacon bits

1. Wash chicken, remove skin, and season chicken with pepper.

2. In a bowl, combine steak sauce and water. Add chicken, cover with plastic wrap, refrigerate until grill is hot. Grill chicken until done, and cut into bite-size pieces.

3. Cook pasta according to package directions. Do not overcook. Drain, toss with olive oil, and refrigerate.

4. In a bowl, combine vinegar, sugar, water, and ranch mix until sugar dissolves. Add oregano, Italian seasoning, tomatoes, cucumbers, celery, and green onions, and toss in cooled pasta. Add Italian dressing and grilled chicken. Refrigerate.

5. Before serving, add shredded cheese and bacon bits and toss well.

Variation: You can also use stir-fried, baked, or broiled chicken. Or try it with turkey.

Chicken and Wild Rice Casserole

Adapted from the recipe by Henrietta Taylor

Yield: 10 to 12 servings

2 (6.2-oz.) pkg. fast-cooking long-grain and wild rice mix

¼ cup butter or margarine

3 celery ribs, chopped

2 medium onions, chopped

2 (8-oz.) cans sliced water chestnuts, drained

5 cups chicken, cooked and chopped into pieces

4 cups (1 lb.) cheddar cheese, shredded and divided

2 (10-oz.) cans cream of mushroom soup, undiluted

2 (8-oz.) pkg. sour cream

1 cup milk

½ tsp. salt

½ tsp. pepper

½ cup soft breadcrumbs

1 (2.25-oz.) pkg. sliced almonds, toasted

1. Preheat the oven to 350°F. Lightly grease a 15×10-inch baking dish.

2. Prepare rice mixes according to package directions.

3. In a large skillet over medium heat, melt butter. Add celery and onion, and sauté 10 minutes or until tender. Stir in water chestnuts, rice, chicken, 3 cups cheese, cream of mushroom soup, sour cream, milk, salt, and pepper.

4. Spoon mixture into the prepared baking dish, and top with breadcrumbs. Bake for 35 minutes. Sprinkle with remaining 1 cup cheese and almonds, and bake for 5 additional minutes.

Note: You can divide this casserole evenly between 2 baking dishes. Bake as directed or freeze casserole up to 1 month. Remove from freezer, and let stand at room temperature for 1 hour. Bake for 55 minutes. Sprinkle with remaining 1 cup cheese and almonds, and bake for 5 additional minutes.

Cheesy Chicken Tetrazzini

Adapted from the recipe by Janis Moats

---

1 small chicken, broth reserved	½ tsp. salt
1 (8-oz.) pkg. spaghetti	½ tsp. pepper
1 stick margarine	1 cup milk
2 cups fresh mushrooms, sliced	3 cups mozzarella cheese, shredded
1 clove garlic, minced	1 cup Parmesan cheese, grated
¼ cup flour	

---

1. In a pot over medium-high heat, add chicken, cover with water, and boil until tender. Debone and shred chicken, and reserve broth.

2. Cook spaghetti in reserved chicken broth. Drain spaghetti in a colander over a pan to retain broth.

3. Melt margarine in large skillet over low heat, add mushrooms and garlic, and sauté for 5 to 10 minutes or until tender. Add flour, salt, and pepper, and stir with a whisk until smooth.

4. Increase the heat to medium, gradually add milk, and continue stirring until sauce thickens. Then gradually add 1½ cups reserved chicken broth, stirring until thickened. Add 2 cups mozzarella and ½ cup Parmesan cheese, and stir until cheese is melted.

5. Place drained spaghetti in a 13×9-inch baking dish. Top with shredded chicken. Pour cheese and mushroom sauce over spaghetti and chicken, and stir until mixture is combined.

6. Bake at 350°F for about 30 minutes or until bubbly. Remove from the oven and top with remaining 1 cup mozzarella cheese and remaining ½ cup Parmesan cheese. Bake for 5 more minutes or until cheese is melted.

Variation: If you want, use 1 cup breadcrumbs instead of cheese for topping. Just spread the breadcrumbs over the mixture and dot with margarine before baking.

Famous Barbecue Chicken

Adapted from the recipe by Jane Knouff

2 TB. vinegar	1 tsp. mustard
2 TB. ketchup	2 TB. butter
1 TB. lemon juice	½ tsp. salt
2 TB. Worcestershire sauce	1 tsp. chili powder
3 TB. brown sugar	1 tsp. paprika
4 TB. water	1 large chicken, cut into pieces

1. Preheat the oven to 500°F.

2. In a large saucepan over medium heat, combine vinegar, ketchup, lemon juice, Worcestershire sauce, brown sugar, water, mustard, butter, salt, chili powder, and paprika. When sauce is heated, place chicken in sauce and coat well.

3. Line a baking dish with aluminum foil and place chicken inside. Seal chicken with the foil.

4. Bake for 15 minutes, reduce the heat to 350°F, and bake for another 1 hour, 15 minutes or until done.

Salsa Chicken

Adapted from the recipe by Danna Namie

Yield: 4 to 5 servings

1 (14-oz.) jar high-quality Mexican salsa	1 tsp. Dijon mustard
2 TB. brown sugar	4 or 5 boneless, skinless chicken breasts

1. In a slow cooker, mix together salsa, brown sugar, and mustard.

2. In a saucepan of water over medium-high heat, boil chicken breasts for 5 minutes. Place chicken in the slow cooker.

3. Cook on high for 1 hour, reduce the heat to low, and cook for 4 hours.

4. Serve chicken on a bed of your favorite rice.

5,000 EGG GIANT OMELETTE CELEBRATION

Abbeville, Louisiana
November
337-893-0013
www.giantomelette.org

According to folklore, Napoleon and his army traveled through southern France, when they came upon the town of Bessieres. The next morning, after spending the night in town, Napoleon feasted on an omelet prepared by the innkeeper. Finding the omelet so delicious, Napoleon asked the townspeople to gather all the eggs in the village and prepare a giant omelet for his army the following day.

In 1984, three members of Louisiana's Abbeville Chamber of Commerce attended the Easter Omelet Festival in Bessieres, France. They also returned home with the determination to bring Abbeville closer to its French heritage by hosting a giant omelet festival.

Today, a famous procession of chefs, eggs, and bread make their way to an enormous 12-foot skillet where the order of the day is preparing a 5,000-egg omelet, which is given away freely to all in attendance. What exactly is in this giant omelet? 5,023+ eggs (1 egg is added each year), 50 pounds onions, 75 bell peppers, 4 gallons onion tops, 2 gallons parsley, 1½ gallons cooking oil, 6½ gallons milk, 52 pounds butter, 3 boxes salt, 2 boxes black pepper, 1 tub crawfish tails, and plenty of Tabasco sauce.

On cooking day, the elected crew rises early to prepare the fire before the giant skillet is positioned. Meanwhile, members of the Giant Omelette Celebration march down the streets of Abbeville greeting the cheering crowd. The procession is a sign the cooking is about to begin. The appointed chefs lead the procession down Concord Street to the giant skillet, where the egg cracking commences.

Of course, no meal in South Louisiana is complete without Tabasco sauce, and the omelet is no exception. The Tabasco Girls are part of the celebration and add a little flavor to the cooking when they dash the Tabasco into the sizzling skillet.

Other than the tasty omelet, many food vendors at the festival prepare and serve up bountiful Cajun fare. Such Bayou treasures include Shrimp on a Stick, Catfish Bites, Crab Balls, Beer-Can Chicken, and Pork Chop Salad.

(5,000 Egg Giant Omelette Celebration)

Omelet Festival's Cajun Omelet

Adapted from the recipe by Kathy Richard

Yield: 1 to 2 servings

5 eggs	2 TB. oil
Salt	2 TB. butter
Pepper	¼ cup onion and bell pepper combined
¼ cup milk	⅓ cup crawfish
Tabasco sauce	¼ cup onion tops and parsley combined

1. Crack eggs into a bowl. Add salt, pepper, milk, and Tabasco sauce. Blend with whisk and then set aside.

2. In a skillet over medium heat, combine oil and butter. Add onion and bell pepper and sauté. Add crawfish and sauté. Add egg mixture to the skillet. Stir gently.

3. Just prior to completion, add onion tops and parsley. Remove the skillet from the heat, and serve with fresh French bread.

The Cajun Way Crawfish Omelet

Adapted from the recipe by the Louisiana Egg Commission

Yield: 4 omelets

1 small onion, diced	1 lb. cooked Louisiana crawfish tails
1 small bell pepper, diced	8 large Louisiana eggs
2 TB. margarine, plus more as necessary	8 TB. water

1. In a sauté pan over medium heat, sauté onion and bell pepper in margarine.
2. Place crawfish tails in a medium bowl and add cooked onion and bell pepper mix.
3. In a separate bowl, beat eggs and water.
4. For each omelet, melt 1 teaspoon margarine in a 10-inch skillet. Add ¼ of omelet mix. Cook for 2 or 3 minutes and then add ¼ of crawfish mix. Season to taste.

Festive Egg Dip

Adapted from the recipe by the Louisiana Egg Commission

Yield: 2 cups

1 (8-oz.) pkg. cream cheese, softened	1 tsp. prepared mustard
½ cup milk	¼ tsp. salt
3 hard-cooked eggs, finely chopped	⅛ tsp. pepper
2 TB. mayonnaise	⅛ tsp. hot pepper sauce
1 TB. chopped chives	

1. In a small mixing bowl, combine cream cheese and milk, and beat with an electric mixer on medium speed until creamy.
2. Add eggs, mayonnaise, chives, mustard, salt, pepper, and hot pepper sauce, mixing until light and fluffy. Serve with crackers or fresh vegetables.

Beer-Battered Fried Shrimp

Adapted from the recipe by the Louisiana Egg Commission

Yield: 6 servings

2 lb. unpeeled large fried shrimp	¼ cup butter or margarine, melted
½ cup all-purpose flour	2 egg yolks
½ cup cornstarch	Vegetable oil
½ tsp. salt	Cocktail sauce
½ cup beer	

---

1. Peel shrimp, leaving tails intact. Devein if desired.

2. In a large bowl, combine flour, cornstarch, and salt. Add beer, butter, and egg yolks, and stir until smooth.

3. Pour 2 inches vegetable oil into a Dutch oven, and heat to 375°F.

4. Dip shrimp into batter and fry, a few at a time, until golden. Drain, and serve with cocktail sauce.

Holland Rusk Pudding

Adapted from the recipe by the Louisiana Egg Commission

Yield: 8 servings

1 (4-oz.) pkg. Rusk Biscuits	3 large eggs, separated
1¼ cups plus 1 TB. sugar	1 tsp. vanilla extract
½ cup unsalted butter, melted	¼ tsp. almond extract
¼ cup all-purpose flour	Sweetened whipped cream
2 cups milk	Apple wedges

1. Preheat the oven to 325°F.

2. Add biscuits to the bowl of a food processor fitted with a metal blade, and process until smooth.

3. Combine biscuit crumbs, ½ cup sugar, and butter. Press ⅔ cup mixture into the bottom of an 11×17-inch baking dish. Reserve remaining crumb mixture.

4. Combine ¾ cup sugar and flour in a heavy saucepan. Stir in milk and egg yolks, and cook over low heat, stirring often, until mixture begins to thicken. Stir in vanilla extract and almond extract.

5. Pour mixture through a large wire-mesh strainer into the baking dish.

6. Beat egg whites with an electric mixer on high speed until foamy. Add remaining 1 tablespoon sugar, beating until stiff peaks form. Spread over custard, and sprinkle with reserved crumb mixture.

7. Bake for 20 to 25 minutes. Cool, and serve with whipped cream and apple wedges.

SEAFOOD

MAINE LOBSTER FESTIVAL

Rockland, Maine
August
1-800-LOB-CLAW (1-800-562-2529)
www.mainelobsterfestival.com

Today, Americans bestow almost ritual status on the consumption of lobster, from the cracking of the shells to the poking of our forks into the plump tail meat to cleansing our fingers with lemon water.

On the East Coast, particularly in Rockland, Maine—the Lobster Capital of the World—residents take their crustacean very seriously. Now in its sixty-first year, the Maine Lobster Festival, nestled on the bustling shore of Rockland's Harbor Park, is the premiere summer food festival in all of New England, attracting more than 100,000 visitors from across the country.

In honor of the great Maine crustacean, the Maine Lobster Festival has it all. The focus is, of course, on fresh, hot Maine lobster. From under the "Maine" Eating Tent—the center of the Festival's dining delights—hungry patrons line up for a single, double, or triple lobster dinner.

During the 5-day festival, nearly 12 tons of luscious lobster are prepared in the world's largest lobster cooker. The gas-fired steamer is capable of cooking several hundred pounds of lobster at one time. Last year, one of the festival volunteers estimated that if you took all the lobsters sold at the festival and placed them end to end, the line of lobsters would equal 13 Empire State Buildings.

In addition to some of the finest lobster you'll find, visitors can sample steamed and fried clams, tender shrimp, steamed mussels, and other Maine seafood, all prepared in the traditional Maine way.

Of course, a food festival cannot be complete without a cooking contest. Amateur cooks from Maine are invited to enter the Maine Lobster Festival Seafood Cooking Contest for their 15 minutes of fame. A panel of three food experts judge the finalists' recipes based on creativity, suitability of the seafood to the recipe, appearance, simplicity of preparation/ingredients, and flavor. The recipes may be any dish category but must contain seafood (fresh, frozen, or canned) indigenous to Maine waters.

(Maine Lobster Festival)

Blushing Maine Lobster Cakes

Adapted from the recipe by Nancy Thompson

Yield: 8 lobster cakes

Olive oil	2 TB. diced pimientos
2 eggs	2 TB. finely chopped chives
2 TB. plus 2 tsp. ketchup	1 lb. lobster meat, cooked and chopped
2 TB. plus ½ cup mayonnaise	1 cup crushed butter crackers
2 TB. butter, melted	1 tsp. lemon juice
1 tsp. seasoned salt	½ tsp. garlic powder
½ tsp. paprika	

---

1. Preheat the oven to 425°F. Oil a cookie sheet with olive oil.

2. In a medium bowl, lightly beat eggs with a wire whisk. Whisk in 2 tablespoons ketchup, 2 tablespoons mayonnaise, butter, ½ teaspoon seasoned salt, and paprika. Stir in pimientos and chives. Add lobster meat and ½ cup crushed butter crackers, and stir gently to combine.

3. Form mixture into 8 cakes, using a ⅓-cup measure for each. Dredge both sides of cakes in remaining ½ cup cracker crumbs, and place on the prepared cookie sheet. Flatten slightly to make a 3-inch cake. Bake for 8 minutes, carefully turn each cake, and bake for another 8 minutes.

4. Combine remaining ½ cup mayonnaise, remaining 2 teaspoons ketchup, lemon juice, garlic powder, and remaining ½ teaspoon seasoned salt in a small bowl, and stir until smooth. Drizzle Rosey Sauce over cakes or serve on the side.

Seafood Chowder

Adapted from the recipe by Jennifer Bouchard

---

6 oz. slab bacon, cut into ½-inch pieces	Salt and freshly ground black pepper
2 TB. butter	½ lb. shucked clams
2 large onions, diced (about 4 cups)	½ lb. haddock, cut into ¾-in. chunks
¼ cup flour	½ lb. Maine shrimp, peeled and deveined
2 or 3 cups clam broth or juice	
4 white potatoes, peeled and diced	½ lb. scallops
2 sweet potatoes, peeled and diced	½ lb. shucked oysters
1½ tsp. dried thyme	4 cups half-and-half
	Fresh parsley

---

1. In a large stockpot over medium heat, cook bacon until browned. Add butter and onions, and cook for 10 minutes. Add flour and stir until well combined. Add broth and then add white potatoes, sweet potatoes, thyme, salt, and pepper, and bring to a simmer. Cook for 10 minutes or until potatoes are almost fork-tender.

2. Add clams, haddock, shrimp, scallops, and oysters, and simmer for 10 minutes. Add half-and-half and heat through. Do not bring to a boil or chowder will curdle.

3. Just before serving, add parsley.

Saffron Lobster Ramekins

Adapted from the recipe by Margo Bartelho

1½ lb. cooked lobster meat	½ cup chopped fresh parsley
1 TB. Old Bay seasoning	1 cup chopped portobello mushrooms
1 tsp. dry mustard	¾ cup sherry
1 TB. sea salt	4 cups heavy cream
1 tsp. white pepper	2 egg yolks
½ lb. unsalted butter	Few threads saffron, finely crushed
1 shallot, chopped	1 cup Monterey Jack cheese, grated
¼ cup chopped garlic	1 pkg. puff pastry sheets

1. Preheat the oven to 350°F.

2. Chunk lobster meat, and lightly rub with Old Bay, mustard, sea salt, and white pepper. Let stand.

3. In a sauté pan over medium heat, melt butter. Add shallot, garlic, parsley, and mushrooms, and sauté until shallots and garlic are transparent and mushrooms are browned. Add lobster mixture to coat. Add sherry and cook down. Remove the pan from heat and let stand, stirring occasionally.

4. In another sauté pan over medium heat, heat cream until hot. Temper egg yolks with cream, and whisk into mixture. Add few threads saffron, and reduce cream by ½. After cream has fully reduced, whisk in grated cheese until melted. Remove the pan from heat and fold cream mixture into lobster mixture.

5. Fill 4 large ramekins or 6 small individual ramekins with mixture to the top. Cut pastry to fit the ramekin tops, and brush with egg wash. Bake for 10 to 15 minutes or until tops are browned and bubbly.

Note: Tempering is the technique used to blend uncooked eggs into a hot liquid or sauce. Eggs are beaten and a little of the hot mixture is stirred into them to warm (temper) the eggs. Tempering slowly raises the temperature of an egg, without curdling it and without heating it through conventional methods.

Lobster Scampi

Adapted from the recipe by Nancy Thompson

½ stick butter

½ cup garlic olive oil

1 TB. hot pepper oil or 1 tsp. crushed red pepper

16 garlic cloves, minced

1 TB. Dijon mustard

1 tsp. Hungarian paprika

2 TB. Worcestershire sauce

½ cup dry white wine

1 TB. fresh lemon juice

½ lb. cooked lobster meat

1. Melt butter, garlic olive oil, and hot pepper oil in a large pan over low heat. When melted, increase the heat to medium, add garlic, and brown slightly.

2. Whisk in Dijon mustard, Hungarian paprika, Worcestershire sauce, and wine, and simmer gently for 5 minutes.

3. Add lemon juice and lobster, and cook until lobster is heated through. Serve over yellow rice.

Seafood Florentine

Adapted from the recipe by Martha Bouchard

---

1 lb. haddock, cut into bite-size pieces

1 lb. shrimp, peeled and deveined

1 lb. sea scallops, cut into bite-size pieces

2 medium sweet potatoes, peeled, halved, and boiled until fork-tender

1 (9-oz.) bag baby spinach leaves, rinsed and stems removed

4 cups heavy cream

Salt and freshly ground black pepper

1 cup fresh grated Parmesan cheese

Fresh parsley

---

1. Preheat the oven to 350°F. Spray a medium-size casserole dish lightly with baking spray.

2. In a mixing bowl, combine haddock, shrimp, and scallops, and mix well.

3. Slice cooked sweet potatoes very thin, and layer slices in the bottom of the prepared baking dish. Cover with baby spinach leaves. Gently pour 2 cups cream over spinach, and season with salt and pepper. Sprinkle with ¾ cup Parmesan cheese and then add seafood mixture. Cover with remaining 2 cups cream and remaining ¼ cup Parmesan. Bake for 25 to 30 minutes.

4. When ready to serve, garnish lightly with fresh chopped parsley or put a sprig of parsley on the side of the dish.

ISLE OF EIGHT FLAGS SHRIMP FESTIVAL

Fernandina Beach, Florida
May
904-261-3248
www.shrimpfestival.com

At the Isle of Eight Flags Shrimp Festival each May, more than 100,000 people turn out for one of Florida's largest seafood festivals to celebrate the birthplace of the modern shrimp industry, the local fishing community, pirate folklore and legends, and of course, lots and lots of shrimp.

Fernandina Beach on Amelia Island hosts the notable festival. The island is located at the extreme northeastern corner of Florida. Amelia Island is Florida's "Golden Gem," which the French visited, the Spanish developed, the English named, and the Americans tamed. It is the only U.S. city to have been under eight different flags: French, Spanish, English, Patriots, Green Cross of Florida, Mexican, Confederate, and American.

The first Shrimp Festival on Amelia Island was held in 1963 to celebrate the traditional blessing of the shrimp fleet. Today, that very tradition continues. During the 4-day sea and seafood event, the Isle of Eight Flags Shrimp Festival serves up a variety of shrimp delicacies. More than 30 vendors batter, fry, sauté, bake, broil, grill, and plate hundreds of pounds of fresh shrimp, along with a variety of other seafood items and homemade tartar sauces. Guests find themselves dining on the tasty bounties of the sea while admiring the commercial shrimp boats, which compete in an offshore race. According to the captains of the vessels, each will sacrifice his or her boat for the love of sport and festival.

Festival attendees can also find a pirate contest for kids, the best-decorated shrimp boat, arts and crafts, a fitness run, and the Miss Shrimp Festival beauty pageant.

Wild Caught Shrimp and Blue Crab Stew

Adapted from the recipe by Janie G. Thomas

Yield: 18 quarts

1 gal. crushed tomatoes	3 lb. whole small yellow onions
1 gal. water	5 lb. whole small red potatoes
1 lemon, sliced thin	3 lb. yellow corn on cob (24 halves frozen), cut in 2-in. pieces
1 lime, sliced thin	
½ cup Old Bay seasoning	1½ doz. cleaned blue crabs, claws cracked, ¼ body, and legs intact
3 lb. Polish kielbasa sausage, cut into 1-in. slices	3 lb. medium (36/40s) wild caught shrimp, heads off

1. In a large pot over high heat, bring tomatoes, water, lemon slices, lime slices, and Old Bay seasoning to a boil. Add sausage, onions, and potatoes.

2. Reduce heat and simmer 20 minutes. Add corn. Continue to simmer for 10 minutes, and add crabmeat. Simmer 10 more minutes, and bring to a boil.

3. Peel, devein, and leave tails on shrimp. Add shrimp to stew, and stir well. Reduce heat to warm, cover, and let stand 1 hour while shrimp steam.

4. Serve stew in bowls with hush puppies.

Wild Caught Shrimp
Low Country Boil

Adapted from the recipe by Janie G. Thomas

Yield: 8 servings

1 gal. water	12 whole new potatoes, cut in ½
Old Bay seasoning	6 corn cobs (fresh or frozen), cut in ½
Salt	12 whole blue crabs, backs removed, and cleaned
4 lemons, sliced thin	
2 lb. "real" smoked sausage or kielbasa or Andouille, sliced ¼-in. thick	2 or 3 lb. wild caught shrimp (minimum ¼ lb. per person)

1. In a large, 20-quart pot (with a basket, if you have one), bring water to a boil. Add Old Bay seasoning, salt, lemon slices, and sausage. Boil 5 minutes, and add potatoes. Boil 5 minutes, and add corn and crabs. Boil 10 minutes, and add shrimp. Continue to boil only until shrimp are done.

2. Quickly remove contents from water (here's where the basket comes in handy), and spread on a newspaper-lined table or counter. Place in large bowls with juice, and serve with hard rolls for dipping.

Wild Caught Shrimp Fried

Adapted from the recipe by Janie G. Thomas

Yield: 2 servings

1 lb. (16 to 18) wild caught shrimp	1 garlic clove, chopped
½ cup House-Autry Breader mix	Cooking wine (optional)
1 stick butter	

1. Remove heads from shrimp, peel, devein, and butterfly with a sharp knife. Keep shrimp cold. (No need to rewash.)

2. Add breader mix to a resealable plastic bag, add 4 shrimp, shake, and remove excess mix. Place shrimp on parchment paper until all shrimp are breaded.

3. In a large, heavy skillet over medium heat, melt butter with chopped garlic. When hot, add all shrimp flat in the pan, side by side. Increase heat to high and cook until brown, about 2 minutes. Turn each shrimp over and brown other side for about 2 minutes more.

4. Deglaze skillet with small amount of cooking wine (if using). Pour over shrimp, and serve shrimp immediately while hot.

Wild Pickled Shrimp

Adapted from the recipe by Janie G. Thomas

1 qt. water	¾ cup white vinegar
2½ lb. shrimp	2½ TB. capers and juice
¼ cup pickling spice	2½ tsp. celery seed
½ cup celery, chopped	Dash Tabasco sauce
5 tsp. salt	2 cups Spanish onions, sliced
1 bay leaf	Bay leaves
1¼ cups salad oil	

1. In a large stockpot over high heat, combine water, shrimp, pickling spice, celery, 3½ teaspoons salt, and bay leaf. Bring to boil, simmer 5 minutes, and cool.

2. Remove shrimp, peel, and devein. Set aside.

3. In a large mixing bowl, combine salad oil, vinegar, capers with juice, celery seed, remaining 1½ teaspoons salt, and Tabasco sauce. Mix well and set marinade aside.

4. In a large glass bowl, alternate layers of onions, shrimp, and bay leaves. Pour marinade over all, and chill at least 24 hours, stirring twice. Keep chilled until ready to serve. Pickled shrimp will keep in refrigerator up to 1 week.

Wild Caught Shrimp Mold

Adapted from the recipe by Janie G. Thomas

---

1 (10-oz.) can tomato soup

1 (8-oz.) pkg. cream cheese

1 (.25-oz.) pkg. unflavored gelatin

1 lb. small wild caught shrimp

1 cup celery, finely chopped

1 cup bell pepper, finely chopped

1 cup green onions, finely chopped

1 cup mayonnaise

---

1. Place tomato soup, cream cheese, and gelatin in a glass bowl, and microwave on low until warm, about 2 minutes. Cool completely. (This mixture must be smooth; use mixer if necessary.)

2. In a pot of water, boil shrimp until done (shrimp will turn pink; do not use any salt or seasonings). Leave heads intact, and peel and finely chop shrimp.

3. In a large mixing bowl, add celery, bell pepper, green onions, and mayonnaise. Add tomato soup mixture and chopped shrimp. Stir to combine.

4. Spray a shrimp-shape gelatin mold with cooking oil spray. Pour in shrimp mixture and refrigerate at least 24 hours.

5. Unmold and serve with crackers.

BREAUX BRIDGE CRAWFISH FESTIVAL

Breaux Bridge, Louisiana
May
337-332-6655
www.bbcrawfest.com

When you think of Louisiana, you can't help but think about crawfish. When crawfish are in season, it's hard to go anywhere in the state without encountering them. That's because Louisiana is the gateway to succulent crawfish and one of the most famous food festivals of all ... the Breaux Bridge Crawfish Festival.

Held every year in May, the festival, dedicated solely to crawfish, attracts thousands of visitors. Thanks to its overwhelming success, hundreds of thousands of dollars generated from the festival have been donated to civic organizations and city improvements around town.

Without question, the Breaux Bridge Crawfish Festival is a pillar in the community. For the past 5 years, it is the recipient of Louisiana's Food Festival of the Year and has received a long list of awards for its marketing campaigns. The festival is so well known that it has attracted reporters from CNN, ABC, NBC, CBS, the Food Network, and PBS. The festival has also been featured in *Southern Living*, *National Geographic*, *The New York Times*, *Country Cooking*, *Motorhome Living*, and *Better Homes and Gardens*. Recently, the Breaux Bridge Crawfish Festival was named a top 10 Food Festival by *USA Today*.

And the festival's crawfish aren't too bad, either. There's a Crawfish Eating Contest, Cajun Cooking Demonstrations, and a Crawfish Étouffée Cook-Off for serious crawfish lovers. Crawfish Races, a crowned Crawfish Queen, and plenty of Cajun music and dancing round out the 3-day festival.

According to Louisiana Fine Foods Company, a wholesale seafood distributor serving restaurants, grocery stores, and other related food industries throughout the United States, there are about 250 species of crawfish found throughout the United States, but only a handful are commercially harvested. Of those harvested, 90 percent are the red swamp and white river crawfish in Louisiana. The large Louisiana crawfish are immediately shipped to the live market, while smaller ones are packed off for meat picking. And it's not just Louisiana natives who love crawfish. The largest foreign market for U.S. crawfish is Sweden, which imports about 2,500 tons of the little critters each year.

(Breaux Bridge Crawfish Festival)

Crawfish Cornbread

Adapted from the recipe by the Breaux Bridge Crawfish Festival

1 cup white cornmeal	2 eggs
½ tsp. baking soda	½ lb. grated cheddar cheese
1 tsp. salt	3 jalapeño peppers, chopped
¼ cup cooking oil	1 cup chopped onions
1 (15-oz.) can cream-style corn	1 lb. chopped cooked crawfish

1. Preheat the oven to 350°F. Lightly grease a 8×10-inch baking pan.

2. In a large mixing bowl, combine cornmeal, baking soda, salt, cooking oil, corn, eggs, cheddar cheese, jalapeño peppers, onions, and crawfish.

3. Pour mixture into the prepared pan, and bake for 45 minutes.

Crawfish Étouffée

Adapted from the recipe by the Breaux Bridge Crawfish Festival

Yield: 4 servings

1 lb. crawfish tails and fat	1 TB. cornstarch
1 or 2 onions, chopped	½ tsp. salt
½ cup butter	1 tsp. Creole seasoning
1 cup water	

1. Heat a large pot over high heat for 10 minutes. Add crawfish, and brown for about 5 minutes. Remove crawfish from the pot, and set aside.

2. Add onions and butter to the pot and sauté until onions are clear.

3. In a small bowl, combine water and cornstarch. Add to butter and onions. Add salt and Creole seasoning.

4. Return crawfish to pot and simmer for 10 to 15 minutes, adding water as needed. Serve over rice.

Crawfish Fettuccine

Adapted from the recipe by the Breaux Bridge Crawfish Festival

Yield: 16 servings

1½ cups margarine

3 medium onions, chopped fine

2 medium bell peppers

¼ cup flour

¼ cup dried parsley

3 lb. crawfish tails

2 pt. half-and-half

1 lb. Velveeta cheese, cut into small pieces

1 lb. jalapeño cheese, cut into small pieces

2 cloves garlic, mined

Salt and red pepper

2 (16-oz.) pkg. fine fettuccine noodles

Parmesan cheese

1. Preheat the oven to 350°F.

2. Melt margarine in large saucepan over medium heat. Add onions and bell peppers, and cook for 10 to 15 minutes or until vegetables are tender.

3. Add flour, cover, and cook approximately 15 minutes, stirring frequently to prevent sticking.

4. Add parsley and crawfish, and cook, covered, for 15 minutes, stirring frequently.

5. Add half-and-half, Velveeta cheese, jalapeño cheese, garlic, salt, and red pepper. Cover and cook on low until cheese melts, stirring occasionally.

6. Cook fettuccine according to package directions. Drain, add to crawfish mixture, and mix thoroughly.

7. Pour mixture into a 10×17×2-inch baking dish, and sprinkle top with Parmesan cheese. Bake for 35 to 40 minutes.

Fried Crawfish Tails

Adapted from the recipe by the Breaux Bridge Crawfish Festival

Yield: 4 servings

2 eggs	1 lb. peeled crawfish tails
1 small can condensed milk	Creole seasoning
1 TB. baking powder	Cooking oil
2 TB. vinegar	1 cup flour

1. In a medium bowl, combine eggs, milk, baking powder, and vinegar.

2. Season crawfish tails with Creole seasoning, and marinate in egg-milk mixture for at least 1 hour.

3. In a large pot, heat cooking oil to 380°F.

4. Remove tails from batter, dip each tail in flour, and deep-fry until golden brown.

Crawfish Pie

Adapted from the recipe by the Breaux Bridge Crawfish Festival

1 onion, chopped	1 lb. cooked crawfish, seasoned
1 bell pepper, chopped	1 (10-oz.) can cream of mushroom soup
½ cup margarine	3 (14-oz.) cans crescent roll dough

1. Preheat the oven to 350°F. Grease a rectangular baking dish.

2. In a sauté pan over medium heat, sauté onion and bell pepper in margarine. Add crawfish and cook for 10 minutes. Add cream of mushroom soup, and mix thoroughly.

3. Layer 3 sections of crescent roll dough on the bottom of the prepared baking dish, and pinch sides of dough along the side of the pan.

4. Add crawfish mixture on top of dough, and cover with remaining 3 sections of dough, pinching sides together. Bake for 10 to 15 minutes or until dough is golden brown.

Judge's Form

Name of Recipe _____

Entrant's Name _____

YARMOUTH CLAM FESTIVAL

Yarmouth, Maine
July
207-846-3984
www.clamfestival.com

Every summer in the charming coastal village of Yarmouth, Maine, locals and visitors from across the country come together for the annual Yarmouth Clam Festival. This summertime tradition is best known for its music and arts, events and competitions, and of course, delicious food.

Freshly harvested clams from the cool Maine waters are brought in where they are eaten raw, steamed, boiled, baked, and fried. Just take a look at some of these marvelous items served up at the festival: whole fried clams in crumbs, fried clam strips, clam chowder, fried calamari, fried oysters, fried shrimp, haddock fingers, lobsters, steamed clams, fried clams in batter, clam cakes, lobster rolls, crabmeat rolls, crab cakes, scallop rolls, tuna salad rolls—the list goes on. The non-seafood lover can find plenty of veggie burgers, gazpacho, and home-baked cheesecakes and peach shortcakes.

Without question, the Yarmouth Clam Festival has been Maine's favorite summer event for more than 40 years. Best of all, admission to the highly celebrated clam festival events is free, including the arts and crafts shows, festival parade, fun run for kids, 5-mile road race for adults, and exciting canoe and kayak races. Proceeds from the food booths and parking lots help support more than 35 nonprofit groups in the town of Yarmouth.

One of the most popular events at the Yarmouth Clam Festival is the Celebrity Clam Shucking Contest featuring local personalities. There's also a Maine State Clam Shucking Contest for both professionals and amateurs. Prizes are awarded for the fastest shuckers. If you think you have what it takes to shuck a clam, or perhaps you've been craving a basket of freshly steamed clams, the Yarmouth Clam Festival is definitely the place to be.

(Yarmouth Clam Festival)

(Mike Leonard)

Clam Chowder

Adapted from the recipe by Ed and Sue Ferrell

¼ cup diced bacon	1 TB. clam base
1 medium onion, diced	1 tsp. thyme
2 stalks celery, diced	1 bay leaf
1 cup diced potatoes	Pinch dried oregano
2 TB. butter	Pinch white pepper
½ cup flour	Heavy cream
1 (12-oz.) can chopped clams	

1. In a large pot over medium heat, add bacon and brown slightly. Add onion, celery, and potatoes. Add butter and cook until onions and celery are soft. Add flour, clams, clam base, thyme, bay leaf, oregano, and white pepper. Cook on low heat until thickened.

2. Stir in heavy cream, and cook chowder until desired thickness. Remove bay leaf and serve immediately.

Clam Dip

Adapted from the recipe by Chef Brian Tebben

½ lb. diced smoked bacon

1 onion, diced

1 bell pepper, diced

2 shallots, diced

2 garlic cloves, diced

1 cup Madeira wine

1 cup Boursin cheese

1 cup cream cheese

Juice of 1 lemon

1 bunch scallions

1½ cups minced clams

Ritz cracker crumbs

Salt and pepper

1. Preheat the oven to 350°F.

2. In a frying pan over low heat, add bacon and cook slowly to crisp bacon without burning. Add onion, bell pepper, shallots, and garlic. Cook until onions are translucent, and deglaze with Madeira. Remove the pan from heat and let contents cool in the pan.

3. In a separate bowl, mix Boursin, cream cheese, lemon juice, scallions, and clams. Stir in cooled pepper and bacon mixture. Pour into a 9x14 baking dish, and top with cracker crumbs. Bake for 10 to 12 minutes or until golden brown.

Spicy Mahogany Clams with Native Wilted Greens

Adapted from the recipe by Chef Stephanie Brown

Yield: 4 servings

6 lb. mahogany clams	5 fresh basil leaves
2 TB. thinly sliced shallots	Salt and pepper
1 cup fresh halved grape or cherry tomatoes	Red pepper flakes
3 TB. butter	Tabasco sauce
¼ cup white wine	1 lb. (16 oz.) pasta
4 large leaves Swiss chard, roughly chopped	½ cup Romano cheese

1. Rinse clams thoroughly under cold water.

2. Heat a large sauté pan over medium-high heat. Add shallots, tomatoes, butter, wine, Swiss chard, basil, salt, pepper, red pepper flakes, and Tabasco sauce. Bring to a boil, add clams, and cover tightly.

3. When all clams have opened, pour over pasta. (Discard any clams that did not open.) Garnish with grated Romano cheese, and serve.

PENN COVE MUSSEL FESTIVAL

Coupeville, Washington
March
360-678-1100
www.penncovemesselfestival.com

The Penn Cove Mussel Festival was founded in 1986 by the Captain Whidbey Inn to celebrate the wonderful Penn Cove mussel. Today, the picturesque town of Coupeville, Washington, known for its numerous festivals and historic downtown located on the scenic waters of Penn Cove, has made the Penn Cove Mussel Festival its own. The first in a series of delightful small-town celebrations, the Penn Cove Mussel Festival gathers the community around one of its most famous treasures—the Penn Cove mussel.

Harvested on the same rocky shoreline as the inn, the Penn Cove mussel is a delicacy treasured at fine restaurants around the world. Naturally prevalent from Alaska to Washington, the Penn Cove mussel prefers pristine bays where snowmelt keeps the salinity lower than the open ocean. Known as the mussel of choice by discriminating chefs and specialty retail buyers, the Penn Cove mussel is mild in texture and packed with sweet flavor. The mussels are grown to a market size of 2½ to 3 inches in 1 year. The Penn Cove Shellfish Company, also located in Coupeville, is America's oldest and largest mussel farm. The company farms the world-famous Penn Cove mussel, which has won numerous international mussel taste contests.

For amateurs and professionals alike, it's easy to distinguish between farmed and wild mussels in that the shells of wild mussels are rough while farm-raised mussels have a clean, smooth shell.

While attending the Penn Cove Mussel Festival in Coupeville, be sure to sample all the wonderful mussel dishes made from the hundreds of pounds of fresh Penn Cove mussels brought in. Don't skip the winning chowders from the festival's Chowder Cook-Off. There's also a Penn Cove mussel eating contest, enjoyable cooking demonstrations, a mussel recipe contest, art and antique walks, Native American activities, and a scavenger hunt for adults.

Quick Mussels and Mayo Appetizers

Adapted from the recipe by Richard Van Schoick

Yield: 4 to 6 servings

3 or 4 lb. mussels, preferably Penn Cove	1 cup mayonnaise
½ cup white wine	1 TB. Dijon mustard
1 tsp. whole black peppercorns	1 tsp. lemon juice
Pinch thyme	1 tsp. Worcestershire sauce
1 bay leaf	

1. Place debearded mussels, wine, peppercorns, thyme, and bay leaf in a skillet, and cook over high heat for 5 to 7 minutes or until heavily steamed. Cover, shake, and stir occasionally, steaming until mussels open. Discard any mussels that do not open.

2. Drain mussels and discard empty ½ of each mussel shell. Set aside.

3. In a bowl, combine mayonnaise, Dijon mustard, lemon juice, and Worcestershire sauce.

4. Place mussels (still in ½ shell) on a serving platter, spoon mayo sauce over each mussel, and serve immediately. Crusty bread and white wine are always good with this appetizer.

Mussels Tarragon

Adapted from the recipe by Angelina Marino

Yield: 5 or 6 servings

6 lb. mussels, preferably Penn Cove	1 bunch fresh cilantro, chopped
¼ cup olive oil	½ bunch fresh oregano, chopped
1 large onion, minced	¼ cup fresh tarragon, chopped
12 cloves garlic, minced	1 bunch fresh green onion, chopped
½ bottle good medium-bodied red wine, perhaps a Pinot Noir	Quartered lemon and lime wedges
	Crusty garlic bread
1 bunch fresh Italian parsley, chopped	

1. Clean, scrub, and debeard mussels if necessary. Soak mussels in salted water for 30 minutes, and strain 5 minutes before adding to the pot.

2. Heat a large Dutch oven over medium heat and add olive oil. Do not let oil burn.

3. Increase heat to high and add mussels to the Dutch oven. Cover immediately. Stand by and shake the pan every so often, peeking inside to be sure all mussels open.

4. Add onions and garlic, cover the pot, and keep it closed for 2 or 3 minutes. Add red wine, cook for 3 more minutes, and add parsley, cilantro, oregano, and green onion. By this time, mussels should be opened wider. Cover the Dutch oven, remove from heat, and let set for 5 to 10 minutes.

5. Discard any mussels that do not open. Serve the rest with wedges of lemon and lime and crusty garlic bread.

Mussels with Pernod and Basil

Adapted from the recipe by Kirk Francis

Yield: 4 to 6

1 bulb fennel root	1 healthy shot Pernod
5 lb. mussels, preferably Penn Cove	Salt and pepper
3 cloves garlic, sliced	⅔ cup cream
Pinch crushed red pepper	25 to 40 fresh basil leaves
2 TB. olive oil	

1. Using a mandoline or a very sharp knife, slice fennel as thinly as you can.

2. Debeard mussels if necessary.

3. In a skillet large enough to accommodate all ingredients, briefly sauté garlic and red pepper in olive oil. Increase heat to high, and add mussels, Pernod, and fennel. Cover and shake the pan occasionally.

4. When mussels have opened (probably no more than 3 minutes—do not overcook), season with salt and pepper and add cream. Tear basil leaves with your hands and add them to the pan.

5. Remove the pan from heat. Discard any mussels that do not open. Serve the rest at once with cooking liquid and crusty bread.

Cassandra's Spicy Mango Mussels

Adapted from the recipe by Rosie McCabe

Yield: 4 to 6 servings

---

3 or 4 lb. mussels, preferably Penn Cove

1 TB. olive oil, plus more for coating mussels

1 TB. butter

½ small onion, minced

1 shallot, minced

4 garlic cloves, minced

1 fresh stalk lemongrass

1 Kaffir lime leaf

2 TB. ginger, sliced or julienned

3 or 4 whole cloves

3 cardamom seeds

1 whole star anise

1 cup white wine

1 (10-oz.) can chicken broth

½ (5.6-oz.) can unsweetened coconut milk, or ½ cup coconut powder dissolved in cold chicken broth

Sea salt

White pepper

¼ tsp. turmeric

Squeeze of lime juice

1½ tsp. cornstarch (optional)

½ diced mango

½ roasted red pepper (1 oz. jar)

---

1. Wash and debeard mussels, and rub with a little olive oil. Sauté mussels in a large pan with butter and 1 tablespoon olive oil. Add minced onion, shallot, and garlic to the pan.

2. Cut lemongrass* into 1½-inch lengths. Split, mash, and add to the pan.

3. Cut Kaffir lime leaf and add to the pan along with ginger, cloves, cardamom seeds, and star anise.

4. In another pan, add white wine, chicken broth, and coconut milk. Bring to a simmer and reduce. Add wine mixture to mussels. Add sea salt, white pepper, turmeric, and lime juice, and adjust seasonings to taste.

5. Fish out lemongrass and anise if you prefer.

6. Dissolve cornstarch in 2 tablespoons cold chicken broth and add to mussels to thicken. Cover and continue to bubble broth 2 or 3 minutes.

7. In a separate sauté pan, gently heat diced mango and roasted red pepper.

8. Discard any mussels that do not open. Add mango-pepper sauce to mussels, and serve with hot crusty bread (or with sticky rice or over noodles). Garnish with remaining diced mango, roasted red pepper, minced onion, and cilantro.

*When using fresh lemongrass, strip off the tough outer leaves and cut off the bottom root portion. Slice the bulbous end into rings on a diagonal.

Thai Mussels in Curry Broth

Adapted from the recipe by Dan Saul

Yield: 2 to 4 servings

2 tsp. sesame oil	1 TB. Thai red curry paste
2 TB. minced fresh ginger	2 tsp. palm sugar (brown sugar)
2 TB. minced fresh garlic	Juice of ½ lime
2 TB. minced fresh lemongrass	½ cup clam juice
1 TB. fish sauce	2 lb. mussels, preferably Penn Cove, cleaned
1 cup coconut milk	

1. In a large pot over medium heat, add sesame oil. Add ginger, garlic, and lemongrass. Sauté for 1 minute. Add fish sauce, coconut milk, Thai red curry paste, palm sugar, lime juice, and clam juice. Bring to a boil. Add mussels (debeard first if necessary). Cover and steam mussels in broth for 3 to 5 minutes or just until opened.

2. Discard any mussels that do not open. Serve the rest with lime slices (from other half of lime).

DUNGENESS CRAB AND SEAFOOD FESTIVAL

Port Angeles, Washington
October
360-457-6110
www.crabfestival.org

In 1848, the oldest commercial crab fishery on the Pacific Coast began in the small village of Dungeness near Sequim, Washington. Today, that fishery is synonymous with the crab named after the waters it comes from—the Dungeness crab.

The Dungeness crab is distinguished from other crabs by its purple-tinged shell, grayish-brown back, and white-tipped claws. They average 6 or 7 inches across and are known around the world for their wonderful texture, buttery flavor, and sweet white meat. Like all crabs, the Dungeness crab is high in protein and minerals and low in fat. About ¼ of this crab's weight is meat, making it one of the meatiest crabs available. Most of the meat is in the eight legs and two claws, although the body contains plenty as well. Dungeness crabs are best eaten chilled, or they may be warmed by lightly steaming. Melt some garlic butter for dipping, and you've got a marvelous feast.

If you prefer to have someone else do the cooking for you, plan on attending the Dungeness Crab and Seafood Festival in Port Angeles, Washington. Here, visitors will find "waterfront village," a large circus tent that shelters a traditional Dungeness crab feed and the freshest Northwest seafood, including salmon, oysters, mussels, and Native American salmon.

Spreading out from Crab Central, festivalgoers will enjoy a bevy of exciting activities such as Olympic Peninsula wine tasting, professional chef demonstrations, local and musical entertainment, an environmental education and maritime center, children's and Native American program areas, and an enriching agriculture program. Vendor booths round out the festival with fine Olympic Peninsula crafts, enticing packaged foods, organic produce, lavender, and other local products.

(Dungeness Crab and Seafood Festival)

Original Dungeness Crab Bisque

Adapted from the recipe by Toga Hertzog

Yield: 6 servings

1 lb. fresh Dungeness crabmeat	Pinch sugar
¼ cup minced shallots	Fresh cracked pepper
¼ cup chopped garlic	Pinch cayenne
4 TB. butter	Onion powder
2 cups heavy whipping cream	Garlic powder
1 TB. clam base or ¼ cup clam stock	1 cup tomato paste
3 or 4 cups crab stock, from 2 boiled fresh Dungeness crabs	Splash cream sherry
	Chopped fresh dill

1. Pick over crabmeat to remove any lingering shell fragments. Set aside ⅓ of crab for garnish.

2. In a stockpot over low heat, sauté shallots and garlic in butter until softened and caramelized. Add heavy whipping cream, increase heat to high, and reduce bisque for 5 minutes. Add clam base, crab stock, sugar, fresh cracked pepper, cayenne, onion powder, dill, and garlic powder, and simmer for 5 minutes.

3. Reduce heat to low, add tomato paste and cream sherry, and continue to simmer for 15 minutes. Add ⅔ fresh crabmeat and blend together. Continue to slightly simmer for 1 or 2 minutes and garnish with reserved crabmeat and a dash of cayenne.

Dungeness Crab Cakes with Roasted Red Bell Pepper Sauce

Adapted from the recipe by Neil Conklin

Yield: 16 (5-ounce) crab cakes

¾ cup red bell pepper, very finely chopped

¾ cup yellow onion, very finely chopped

¾ cup celery, very finely chopped

1 TB. canola oil

3 cups focaccia breadcrumbs

2½ lb. Dungeness crabmeat

¼ cup Worcestershire sauce

6 shakes Tabasco sauce

1½ cups mayonnaise

1 TB. minced garlic

1 tsp. dried thyme

1 TB. dried parsley

1 tsp. black pepper

1 tsp. dry yellow mustard

1 tsp. Old Bay seasoning

3 roasted red bell peppers, skin and seeds removed

3 cloves roasted garlic

Pinch red pepper flakes

¼ cup olive oil

Salt and pepper

1 cup cream

3 or 4 TB. olive oil

1. Preheat the oven to 350°F.

2. In a sauté pan over medium heat, sauté red bell pepper, yellow onion, and celery in canola oil.

3. Toast thin slices of focaccia bread under the oven broiler until light brown. Pulse toasted focaccia in a food processor until the consistency of fine breadcrumbs.

4. Clean and drain crabmeat and add to a large bowl. Add Worcestershire sauce, Tabasco sauce, mayonnaise, minced garlic, thyme, parsley, black pepper, mustard, and Old Bay seasoning, and mix. Add breadcrumbs until mixture adheres into a ball. If needed, add more mayonnaise to adjust consistency.

5. Form cakes with approximately ¾ cup crab cake mixture, pressing firmly to 1½ inches thick, keeping the sides uniformly round. Sauté in ¼ inch olive oil until brown on both sides.

6. In a food processor, add roasted peppers and purée, slowly adding olive oil, garlic, and red pepper flakes.

7. In a saucepan over medium heat, add purée and cream, and reduce to desired consistency. Season with salt and pepper.

8. Serve crab cakes with Red Bell Pepper Sauce.

Dungeness Crab and Bay Shrimp–Stuffed Salmon

Adapted from the recipe by Bill Graham

Yield: 6 to 8 servings

8 oz. Dungeness crab, with juice	¾ to 1 cup panko crumbs
8 oz. bay shrimp	¾ cup cream cheese, softened
1 egg	Dash Worcestershire sauce
1 heaping TB. chopped fresh parsley	6 to 8 oz. skinless salmon fillets
1 heaping TB. chopped chervil	Garlic butter or olive oil
1½ TB. Dijon mustard	

1. Preheat the oven to 450°F. Grease a baking sheet.

2. In a bowl, blend crab, shrimp, egg, parsley, chervil, and Dijon mustard. Add panko until most of juices have been absorbed. Leave moist, as panko will continue to absorb some juices.

3. Blend softened cream cheese with Worcestershire sauce. Mix together with panko mixture.

4. Cut a small X into the center of each salmon fillet. Fill with about ½ cup stuffing mixture. Brush with garlic butter or olive oil. Bake for 15 to 20 minutes or until salmon is done.

Dungeness Crab
and Bay Shrimp Radiatore

Adapted from the recipe by Bill Graham

Yield: 6 servings

¾ lb. fresh Dungeness crabmeat	Pinch sugar
¼ lb. fresh or frozen bay shrimp, thawed if frozen	Fresh cracked pepper
	Pinch cayenne
¼ cup minced shallots	Splash cream sherry
3 cloves garlic, chopped	Fresh grated Parmesan cheese
4 TB. butter	2 lb. cooked radiatore pasta, rinsed, drained, and oiled
2 cups heavy whipping cream	
1 TB. clam base, or ¼ cup clam stock	Chopped fresh dill

1. Pick over crabmeat to remove any lingering shell fragments. Set aside ⅓ of crab and bay shrimp for garnish.

2. In a sauté pan over low heat, sauté shallots and garlic in butter until softened. Sauté for an additional minute. Add heavy whipping cream, increase heat to high, and reduce sauce for 1 minute. Add clam base, sugar, fresh cracked pepper, and cayenne, and simmer for 2 minutes. Reduce heat to low, add cream sherry, and continue to simmer for 2 minutes. Add grated Parmesan cheese, ⅔ fresh crabmeat, bay shrimp, and cooked radiatore pasta, and continue to simmer. Occasionally toss, blending mixture together.

3. Garnish with reserved crabmeat, bay shrimp, and grated Parmesan cheese, and sprinkle with chopped dill.

Romesco-Crusted Halibut over Wilted Spinach

Adapted from the recipe by Joy Siemion

Yield: 8 servings

1 cup chopped roasted pepper	1 TB. butter
⅛ cup almonds, chopped	1 lb. fresh organic baby spinach
⅛ tsp. chili flakes	2 lemons, halved and juiced
⅛ cup fresh basil	1 cup grated Parmesan
2 cloves garlic, minced	¼ cup gold raisins
¼ olive oil	Lemon zest
Salt and pepper	¼ cup pine nuts
8 fresh halibut fillets	

1. Preheat the oven to 400°F.

2. Add roasted pepper, almonds, chili flakes, basil, garlic, olive oil, salt, and pepper to a food processor and pulse. Set Romesco Sauce aside.

3. In a medium frying pan over high heat, sear halibut for 3 or 4 minutes or until golden brown. Turn, top with Romesco Sauce, and finish cooking in the oven for 5 to 10 minutes.

4. In a sauté pan over medium heat, add butter and cook until brown and slightly nutty in flavor. Add spinach, and toss with tongs until spinach begins to wilt. Add lemon juice, Parmesan cheese, raisins, lemon zest, and pine nuts. Season with salt and pepper, and transfer to a plate.

5. Remove halibut from oven, gently place each fillet over wilted spinach, and serve.

WORLD CATFISH FESTIVAL

Belzoni, Mississippi
April
1-800-408-4838
www.catfishcapitalonline.com

Since the mid-1960s, when catfish was introduced to Mississippi as a new cash crop, to 1976, when the farm-raised catfish industry had an overwhelming impact on the local economy, community leaders of Humphreys County, Mississippi, began looking for new ways to pay tribute to the industry.

As a part of the City of Belzoni Bicentennial Celebration, the first festival, the Bicentennial Catfish Festival, was held in April 1976 on the lawn of the Humphreys County courthouse. Roughly 3,000 people attended the festival, which included a catfish eating contest, a crowned Catfish Queen, musical entertainment, arts and crafts, and plenty of catfish dishes to sample.

Today, the (renamed) World Catfish Festival welcomes more than 20,000 visitors each year to Belzoni, Mississippi—no wonder Humphreys County has been proclaimed the Catfish Capital of the World. Expanding from those days of hosting the festival on the courthouse lawn, the World Catfish Festival now encompasses the entire downtown area, including four streets for the arts and craft show. Events at the festival include the ever-popular Catfish Eating Contest, the Catfish Fry, and the crowning of Miss Catfish. Visitors come from not only Mississippi and across the United States, but from many foreign countries as well. Due in part to its reputation as a family-oriented event, the World Catfish Festival has received numerous awards, including Top 100 Events in North America and Top 20 Events of the Southeast.

The Catfish Institute, which promotes healthy, great-tasting uses for genuine U.S. farm-raised catfish, plays an integral role in the festival's great success. Founded in 1986, this nonprofit organization helps raise awareness of festival attendees about the many culinary benefits of genuine U.S. farm-raised catfish.

Catfish Dip

Adapted from the recipe by the World Catfish Festival

4 (4-oz.) catfish fillets, cooked and flaked	1½ cups sour cream
1 qt. water	⅓ cup Picante sauce
1 (3-oz.) box crab boil	1 (7-oz.) pkg. Italian salad dressing mix
	2 tsp. lemon juice

1. In a deep pan over medium heat, poach catfish fillets in water and crab boil. Drain and flake fillets with a fork.

2. Place flaked catfish in a large mixing bowl. Add sour cream, picante sauce, salad dressing mix, and lemon juice, and mix well. Refrigerate until cool.

3. Serve dip with corn chips, crackers, or celery.

Pecan Catfish

Adapted from the recipe by the World Catfish Festival

Yield: 1 or 2 servings

2 TB. milk	4 (4-oz.) catfish fillets
3 TB. Dijon mustard	1 cup ground pecans

1. Preheat the oven to 500°F. Grease a baking sheet.

2. In a small bowl, combine milk and Dijon mustard. Dip catfish fillets into mustard mixture. Then dip into ground pecans, shaking off excess.

3. Place fillets on the prepared baking sheet. Oven-fry for 10 to 12 minutes or until catfish flakes.

Layered Catfish Appetizer

Adapted from the recipe by the World Catfish Festival

Yield: 12 servings

3 cups water	2 TB. mayonnaise
2 or 3 catfish fillets	1 small onion, chopped fine
12 oz. softened cream cheese	Dash garlic salt
2 TB. Worcestershire sauce	1 small bottle chili sauce
1 TB. lemon juice	Parsley

1. In a large skillet, bring water to boil. Add catfish, return to boil, and reduce heat. Cover and simmer gently for 5 to 7 minutes until fish flakes easily. Remove from water. Cool slightly. Flake catfish; set aside.

2. In a medium bowl, combine cream cheese, Worcestershire sauce, lemon juice, mayonnaise, onion, and garlic salt. Mix well and chill for several hours.

3. When cool, spread cream cheese layer on a round tray. Top with a layer of chili sauce, a layer of flaked catfish, and a sprinkling of parsley. Enjoy with crackers or chips.

Catfish Parmesan

Adapted from the recipe by the World Catfish Festival

Yield: 2 to 4 servings

⅔ cup freshly grated Parmesan cheese	1 egg, beaten
¼ cup all-purpose flour	¼ cup milk
½ tsp. salt	5 or 6 small catfish fillets (about 2 lb.)
¼ tsp. pepper	¼ cup margarine, melted
1 tsp. paprika	⅓ cup sliced almonds

1. Preheat the oven to 350°F. Lightly grease a 13×9×2-inch baking dish.

2. In a medium bowl, combine Parmesan, flour, salt, pepper, and paprika.

3. In a separate bowl, combine egg and milk.

4. Dip catfish fillets in egg mixture and then dredge in flour mixture.

5. Arrange fillets in the prepared baking dish, drizzle with butter, and sprinkle almonds over the top. Bake for 35 to 40 minutes or until fish flakes easily when tested with a fork.

Catfish Vermouth

Adapted from the recipe by the World Catfish Festival

Yield: 1 to 2 servings

3 or 4 (4-oz.) catfish fillets	¼ cup white vinegar
1 TB. lemon pepper seasoning	¼ cup dry vermouth

1. Sprinkle fillets with lemon pepper.

2. In a lidded bowl or a resealable plastic bag, add vinegar and vermouth. Add catfish, and marinate for about 1 hour.

3. In a nonstick skillet over medium heat, simmer catfish 5 minutes per side until all liquid is cooked out and fish is browned.

Lucie's Catfish Supreme

Adapted from the recipe by the World Catfish Festival

Yield: 4 to 6 servings

8 (4-oz.) catfish fillets	1 tsp. garlic powder
Paprika	1 tsp. celery salt
1 (8-oz.) can tomato sauce	1 TB. parsley flakes
1 tsp. lemon pepper seasoning	Parmesan cheese

1. Preheat the oven to 350°F.

2. Sprinkle catfish with paprika and place in a glass baking dish.

3. In a medium bowl, mix tomato sauce, lemon pepper seasoning, garlic powder, celery salt, and parsley flakes. Pour sauce over fish, covering well. Cover the dish with aluminum foil, and bake for 20 minutes.

4. Uncover, sprinkle fish with Parmesan cheese, recover with foil, and bake 5 additional minutes.

5. Uncover again and heat under the broiler for 2 or 3 minutes to brown cheese. Serve immediately.

Catfish Lucie

Adapted from the recipe by the World Catfish Festival

Yield: 2 to 4 servings

4 (4-oz.) catfish fillets	2 TB. white wine
Salt and pepper	Worcestershire sauce
Lemon juice	4 strips bacon
Garlic powder	

---

1. Preheat the oven to 350°F.

2. Rub catfish fillets well with salt and pepper, and place in a shallow baking dish. Squeeze lemon juice over fillets, and sprinkle with garlic powder. Pour white wine over fish along with Worcestershire sauce.

3. Place 1 bacon strip on each fillet, and cover the dish with aluminum foil. Bake 20 minutes.

4. Uncover and bake for 10 to 15 additional minutes. Serve with a green salad and baked potato.

COPPER RIVER WILD SALMON FESTIVAL

Cordova, Alaska
July
907-424-7260
www.copperriverwild.org

Cordova, Alaska, is home to the famous culinary fish, the Copper River salmon, named after the 300-mile Copper River—one of the longest and most rugged rivers in Alaska. King, Sockeye, and Silver salmon embark on an endless journey up the Copper River to spawn and lay their eggs—hence the name Copper River salmon. Because the salmon's journey is so long, they store extra fat and oils in the flesh so they can survive the long trip. This high fat and oil content is why Copper River salmon are recognized as some of the world's best eating salmon. Their bright red flesh, firm texture, and rich flavor make them well sought after—and at the Copper River Wild Salmon Festival in Cordova, this culinary treat is served up in a bevy of styles for hungry festivalgoers.

Join the Copper River Wild Salmon Festival for a weekend full of fun and festivity while experiencing the energy and enthusiasm of this rustic fishing community. Cordova, incidentally, is surrounded by extraordinary ecosystems that combine to form one of the world's most spectacular natural environments and serve as host to a thriving wild salmon migration. Through the wide variety of art, music, road races, and educational events, the Copper River Wild Salmon Festival aims to celebrate salmon and promote the health and sustainability of the local salmon runs.

Thanks to the participation of guest chefs and local volunteers, the festival is proud to host the popular Taste of Cordova: Copper River Salmon Cook-Off, where local residents and visitors compete in preparing the most delectable ethnic salmon dishes. The cook-off is followed by a Happy Hour auction, a Salmon Barbecue, and a Salmon Jam Music Festival.

If you're feeling adventurous and ready to brave the raw and untamed lands we call Alaska, pack your bags and head up to Cordova for the Copper River Wild Salmon Festival.

(Copper River Wild Salmon Festival)

Smoked Salmon Tapenade

Adapted from the recipe by Mimi Briggs

---

4 large Roma tomatoes, seeded and diced

¼ cup green onions, chopped

2 TB. fresh parsley, minced

2 TB. fresh cilantro, minced

4 oz. smoked salmon

3 TB. olive oil

2 TB. capers, with a little juice

1 lemon, juiced

1 lime, juiced

Salt and pepper

---

1. In a large bowl, combine tomatoes, green onions, parsley, cilantro, salmon, olive oil, capers with juice, lemon juice, lime juice, salt, and pepper. Mix well.

2. Refrigerate until ready to serve. Serve with a French baguette sliced into rounds.

Kate's Pan-Fried Copper River Salmon Cakes

Adapted from the recipe by Kate Alexander

1¼ lb. fresh Copper River salmon fillet

1 slice white sandwich bread, crust removed and chopped very fine

2 TB. mayonnaise

¼ cup minced onion

¼ cup diced red pepper

1 tsp. dried parsley

Dash mustard

¾ tsp. salt

1½ TB. lemon juice

½ cup flour

2 eggs, lightly beaten

½ cup plus 1½ tsp. vegetable oil

1½ tsp. water

¾ cup panko breadcrumbs

---

1. Debone, skin, and chop salmon into ¼-inch pieces. Mix salmon with bread, mayonnaise, onion, red pepper, parsley, mustard, salt, and lemon juice. Form into 2½-inch patties, enough for 8 to 10 cakes, and place on a lightly oiled baking sheet. Freeze for about 10 minutes to help firm patties and allow surface moisture to evaporate.

2. In the meantime, spread flour in shallow baking dish.

3. Mix eggs with 1½ teaspoons vegetable oil and water in a second shallow dish.

4. Put breadcrumbs in another shallow bowl.

5. Remove salmon patties from the freezer. One by one, dip each patty in flour, shaking off any excess; coat on all sides in egg mixture, letting any excess drip off; coat completely with breadcrumbs; and return to baking sheet.

6. Heat remaining ½ cup vegetable oil in heavy-bottomed skillet over medium-high heat. Get oil hot but not smoking. Add salmon patties and cook for about 2 minutes per side or until golden brown. Transfer cakes to a plate with paper towels to absorb excess oil, and serve immediately with your favorite dipping sauce.

Saffron Shiitake Risotto Salmon Swirls

Adapted from the recipe by the Copper River Wild Salmon Festival

½ cup onion, minced

½ cup carrot, minced

½ cup celery, minced

Salt and pepper

½ tsp. saffron

3 or 4 TB. olive oil

2 cloves garlic

1 cup rice

½ cup shiitake mushrooms, sliced

½ cup white wine

2½ to 3 cups chicken, vegetable, or fish stock

2 TB. butter

¼ cup half-and-half

¼ cup Parmesan cheese

1 salmon fillet, preferably large Copper River king salmon

1. In a sauté pan over medium-high heat, sauté onion, carrot, celery, salt, pepper, and saffron in oil for 15 minutes. Add garlic and rice, and sauté 3 to 5 minutes. Add wine and boil until almost dry over medium heat.

2. Gradually add stock ½ cup at a time, stirring constantly with a wooden spoon. Boil each ½ cup stock addition until almost dry before adding more. Keep adding stock or additional water until rice is cooked.

3. Finish with butter and half-and-half, and boil until almost dry. Add Parmesan cheese, and set risotto aside to cool.

4. Slice salmon horizontally to create 2 or 3 "sheets" ½-inch thick.

5. Grease large piece of aluminum foil. Arrange salmon in a single layer to cover the foil, and season with salt and pepper. Spoon risotto over fish, and spread into a consistent thin layer.

6. Roll foil with fish and risotto similar to a sushi roller, keeping the foil on the outside. Secure roll with toothpicks as needed.

7. Fry foil roll in a hot pan over high heat, rolling around to cook completely. Fish should be brown and crisp next to the foil. Slice sushi style and remove foil before serving.

Copper River Salmon Thai Curry

Adapted from the recipe by the Copper River Wild Salmon Festival

Yield: 4 to 6 servings

2 (5.6-oz.) cans coconut milk

4 tsp. red or green curry paste

⅓ cup water

1½ cups vegetables (zucchini, Japanese eggplant, and/or yellow squash), cut into ½-in. chunks

4 tsp. palm sugar (brown sugar)

2 TB. soy sauce or fish sauce

1½ lb. wild salmon fillet, skinned and cut into 2-in. chunks

4 Kaffir lime leaves

½ cup fresh Thai basil leaves, removed from stems

1. In a 2½-quart pot over medium-low heat, simmer 1 can coconut milk, without stirring, until coconut oil separates from cream. A bubbly film of coconut oil should coat the surface. (It's better to let it sit too long than too little.)

2. Mix curry paste into coconut milk, and let it sit without stirring for a few more minutes until mixture comes to a boil and film of bubbly oil at the surface reappears.

3. Mix in remaining can coconut milk and water, increase heat to medium, and bring to a boil.

4. Add vegetables, and stir in palm sugar and soy sauce. Simmer until vegetables are cooked to desired tenderness.

5. Remove the pot from heat, and stir in salmon, Kaffir lime leaves, and basil. Cover the pot and let sit for 5 minutes.

6. Pour curry into serving bowls over steamed white rice, and garnish with fresh basil.

Part 3

Fruits, Nuts, and Vegetables

BAYFIELD
APPLE FESTIVAL

Bayfield, Wisconsin
October
717-677-9413
www.bayfield.org/visitor/applefestival.asp

Bayfield, Wisconsin's Apple Festival is celebrating more than 45 years of food, fun, and entertainment. Named one of the "Top Ten Autumn Festivals in North America" by the Society of American Travel Writers, and touted by *Wisconsin Trails* magazine as Wisconsin's best festival, the Bayfield Apple Festival attracts more than 60,000 visitors to the picturesque town of fewer than 700 people.

Nestled on the shores of Lake Superior, Bayfield has earned a reputation as a colorful, charming, and friendly community. Recently, a writer for the *Chicago Tribune* spent weeks on the road in search of "The Best Little Town in the Midwest." Bayfield was his top choice.

Bayfield is also home to many commercial flower farms, berry farms, and orchards, where visitors can walk among the crops; savor the beauty; and pick pails of apples, raspberries, strawberries, blackberries, and blueberries.

The popular Bayfield Apple Festival is proud to feature more than 45 orchards and food booths selling Bayfield apples, apple desserts, and delicacies over the course of 3 days. There's plenty to buy and see, including more than 150 arts-and-crafts booths. Also not to be missed is a Venetian Boat Parade, comprised of glimmering boats decorated with lights, a grand parade featuring Bayfield's exclusive 600-member "Mass Band," a traditional fish boil dinner, musical entertainment, ongoing street performers throughout the festival grounds, and an evening dance.

Contests are another highlight at the festival. Apple lovers of all ages participate in the festival's annual apple pie and dessert contests. There's also an Apple Dumpling Gang contest for the little ones. Think you're good at peeling an apple? Try the apple-peeling contest, where contestants complete to produce the longest apple peel. Paula Collins, who has been participating in the contest for more than 12 years, once produced a peel measuring more than 18 feet long! She won.

(*Knowles Communications.com*)

Apple Cheddar Muffins

Adapted from the recipe by Pinehurst Inn at Pikes Creek, Bayfield, Wisconsin

Yield: 12 muffins

1 large Haralson or Golden Delicious apple	½ tsp. salt
1½ cups unbleached, organic flour	1 tsp. cinnamon
¼ cup regular oatmeal, uncooked	¾ cup buttermilk
2 TB. sugar	2 eggs (local, organic preferred)
2 tsp. baking powder	¼ cup unsalted butter, melted
½ tsp. baking soda	¾ cup finely grated cheddar cheese

1. Preheat the oven to 400°F. Butter standard muffin tins.

2. Peel, halve, and core apple, and shred or dice to small pieces. Set aside.

3. In a large bowl, combine flour, oatmeal, sugar, baking powder, baking soda, salt, and cinnamon. Set aside.

4. In a medium bowl, whisk together buttermilk, eggs, and melted butter until smooth. Stir in diced apple and cheese. Add to dry ingredients, and stir just until blended.

5. Spoon batter into the muffin tins, filling each cup about ¾ full. Bake for about 20 minutes or until a toothpick inserted into center of muffins comes out clean. Cool in the tins for at least 5 minutes before removing.

Apple-Glazed Pork Chops

Adapted from the recipe by the Bayfield Apple Festival

Yield: 6 servings

6 (1-lb.) pork chops, center cut (each about 2 in. thick)

4 TB. vegetable oil

3 cups reduced pork broth (see step 4)

½ cup dry red wine

1 tsp. freshly minced thyme

1 tsp. freshly minced marjoram

1 tsp. freshly minced basil

1 tsp. freshly minced summer savory

1 TB. minced fresh garlic

4 TB. flour

5 TB. cold water

Apple Cider Marmalade:

5 cups Cortland or other type apples, unpeeled, cored, and slivered

1 cup apple cider

1 cup orange juice concentrate

½ cup orange zest

½ cup lemon zest

1 (1.75-oz.) pkg. pectin

7 cups sugar

1. Preheat the oven to 325°F.

2. In a heavy, preheated skillet, brown pork chops in vegetable oil over medium heat for 10 minutes per side or until well browned.

3. Arrange chops in a roasting pan. Pour pork broth and wine over chops. Add thyme, marjoram, basil, summer savory, and garlic. Cover and bake for 2 or 3 hours or until fork tender. When pork chops are done, remove chops from the oven and keep warm.

4. Strain pan juices and skim off fat. Measure 3 cups pan juices and transfer to a saucepan.

5. Blend flour and water in small bowl until smooth. Whisk into pan juices. Cook brown sauce over medium heat until thickened. Reduce heat to low and simmer 3 minutes, stirring occasionally.

6. Place apples, cider, orange juice concentrate, orange zest, lemon zest, and pectin in a large saucepan or jelly kettle over medium-high heat. Bring mixture to a rolling boil.

7. Add sugar and stir until completely dissolved. Bring to a rolling boil again, and boil 65 seconds, stirring constantly. Remove mixture from heat, and cool for 3 minutes.

8. Skim off any foam with a slotted spoon. Pour marmalade into sterilized jars, seal, and process in a water bath according to jar manufacturer's instructions.

9. Ladle brown sauce onto a warm plate. Arrange a pork chop in the center of each plate, and spoon warm apple cider marmalade over each chop.

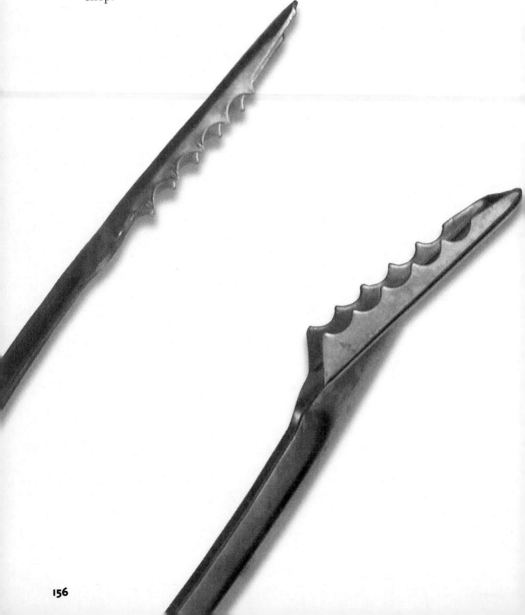

Bayfield Apple Festival's Apple Pie

Adapted from the recipe by Sharon Locey

Yield: 1 pie

1¾ cups flour	1½ cups sugar
1 tsp. salt	1 tsp. cinnamon
¼ tsp. baking powder	8 cups Wealthy apples, peeled and sliced
½ cup vegetable oil	1½ tsp. lemon juice
3 TB. ice water	¼ cup margarine

1. Preheat the oven to 450°F.

2. In a mixing bowl, combine flour, salt, baking powder, and oil, and mix until crumbly. Add ice water, and stir dough into a ball. Wrap in saran wrap and chill for at least ½ hour.

3. Divide dough into 2 pieces. Roll out one piece (until 12 inches in diameter) between 2 sheets of fresh waxed paper. Roll the next piece to 9 inches in diameter. Place the 9-inch piece in a pie pan, trimming any extra dough from the edges with a sharp knife.

4. In another bowl, mix sugar and cinnamon, and toss with apples. Pour apples into the pie pan, and drizzle lemon juice over top. Dot apples with slices of margarine. Add 12-inch dough piece to cover the top, using a fork or your fingers to pinch the edges together. Cut a couple slits in the top.

5. Bake for 15 minutes. Reduce the temperature to 350°F and bake for 45 more minutes.

Glazed Fresh Apple Cookies

Adapted from the recipe by Muriel Erickson

4½ cups flour

1 tsp. ground cloves

1 tsp. ground nutmeg

2 TB. cinnamon

1⅛ tsp. salt

1 cup shortening

2 tsp. baking soda

2⅔ cups brown sugar

2 eggs

1 cup plus 2½ TB. apple cider, orange juice, or milk

2 cups Jonathan apples, unpeeled and finely chopped

1 cup raisins

1 or 2 cups chopped pecans or walnuts

1 TB. butter

1½ cups confectioners' sugar

¼ tsp. vanilla extract

---

1. Preheat the oven to 375°F. Grease a cookie sheet using a napkin or paper towel.

2. In a mixing bowl, sift together flour, cloves, nutmeg, cinnamon, baking soda, and 1 teaspoon salt.

3. In a separate bowl, cream together shortening and brown sugar. Add eggs, 1 cup apple cider, and chopped apples. Add dry ingredients, and fold in raisins and nuts.

4. Drop cookies by the spoonful onto the prepared cookie sheet. Bake for 10 minutes per batch.

5. While cookies bake, make glaze. In a bowl, cream butter, confectioners' sugar, and remaining ⅛ teaspoon salt. Stir in 2½ tablespoons apple cider and vanilla extract. (If using orange juice, do not use vanilla extract.)

6. Glaze cookies while hot, and remove from cookie sheet.

Caramel Apple Crisp

Adapted from the recipe by Janine Johnson

8 cups Cortland or Honey Crisp apples, peeled and sliced

¼ cup sugar

2 tsp. cinnamon

1 cup brown sugar

1 cup quick-cooking oatmeal

½ tsp. salt

1 cup plus 2 TB. flour

1 stick butter

½ (5.5-oz.) bag caramels

¼ cup cream

1. Preheat the oven to 400°F.

2. Spray a 9×13 pan with nonstick cooking spray, and arrange apples in the pan.

3. In a bowl, mix sugar and 1 teaspoon cinnamon. Sprinkle cinnamon mixture over top of apples.

4. Mix brown sugar, oatmeal, salt, flour, butter, and remaining 1 teaspoon cinnamon, and sprinkle over top of apples. Bake crisp for 45 to 50 minutes.

5. In a bowl, microwave caramels with cream until melted and smooth. Pour topping over apple crisp.

CALIFORNIA STRAWBERRY FESTIVAL

Oxnard, California
May
1-888-288-9242
www.strawberry-fest.org

Every May in Oxnard, California, strawberry devotees unite for the city's delicious California Strawberry Festival, a 2-day, all-around celebration serving up a menu of spectacular strawberry delights, along with endless entertainment. Presented by the all-volunteer California Strawberry Festival Executive Board, the strawberry tribute provides visitors with plenty of festival fun. Stroll through and experience a 12-foot-long strawberry field "Life of a Strawberry" exhibit. At the top of every hour, the Promenade's presenter stage comes alive with enlightening activities and workshops like quick-and-easy strawberry recipes for people on the go, health and wellness strawberry style, and proper care for your own strawberry garden.

There's also Strawberryland for Kids, arts and crafts, a climbing wall, bungee jumping, gooey contests for berry lovers, and plenty of lip-smacking strawberry treats. Popular favorites at the more than 50 on-site food booths include chocolate-dipped strawberries, strawberry shortcakes (where more than 10,000 pounds of sliced strawberries and 250 flats of whole strawberries are served), strawberry pizza, strawberry egg rolls, strawberry kabobs, strawmonade, and even BBQ sandwiches with sweet strawberry sauce.

A highly anticipated annual pre-event tradition is for people to send in their favorite recipes using strawberries as the central theme. Three finalists are selected to prepare their dishes for the cook-off and final judging, which is based on taste, originality, preparation, best use of strawberry, and presentation.

Ever wonder how many strawberries you might devour in a matter of seconds or what it might feel like to have strawberry tarts thrown in your face? If such thoughts have crossed your mind, be sure to enter the messy contests that get everyone into the act. Peer through cut-outs on a large board painted with a bowl of strawberries at the Strawberry Tart Toss and become a target while fellow contestants take aim with strawberry tarts. Over at the Strawberry Shortcake Eating Contest, your hearty appetite is put to the test as you attempt to devour a bowl of strawberry shortcake complete with whipped cream and all the fixings.

(California Strawberry Festival)

Strawberry Muffins

Adapted from the recipe by the California Strawberry Festival

Yield: Approximately 12 muffins

1½ cups all-purpose flour	¼ cup butter, melted
½ cup plus 1 TB. sugar	3 TB. whole milk
2½ tsp. baking powder	1 large egg, lightly beaten
1½ tsp. cinnamon	½ cup high-quality strawberry jam
¼ tsp. salt	½ cup fresh, ripe California strawberries, mashed
⅔ cup vanilla yogurt	

1. Preheat the oven to 375°F.

2. In a large bowl, combine flour, ½ cup sugar, baking powder, 1 teaspoon cinnamon, and salt, and stir well with a whisk. Make a well in the center of mixture.

3. In another bowl, combine yogurt, butter, milk, and egg, stirring well with a whisk. Add yogurt mixture to flour mixture, stirring just until moist.

4. Spray foil muffin cups with vegetable cooking spray, and place them into the muffin pan. Spoon 1 tablespoon batter into each cup, and top with 1 teaspoon freshly mashed strawberries. Top evenly with remaining batter.

5. In a small bowl, combine remaining 1 tablespoon sugar and remaining ½ teaspoon cinnamon, and sprinkle over batter.

6. Bake muffins for 15 minutes or until a toothpick inserted in the center comes out clean. Cool muffins on a wire rack for 15 minutes and then remove from the pan.

Brie and Pear Salad
with Strawberry Cream Dressing

Adapted from the recipe by Kathi Hopkins

Yield: 4 servings

1 small round Brie cheese	¼ cup raspberry vinegar
4 pears, cored and peeled	¾ cup nonfat sour cream
3 cups fresh, ripe California strawberries	1 TB. high-quality strawberry preserves
Romaine lettuce (or your favorite salad greens)	

1. Slice Brie into bite-size pieces.

2. Slice pears vertically.

3. Slice 1 basket worth of strawberries.

4. Divide romaine among 4 plates. Top with sliced pears and cheese. Arrange strawberry slices around salad and atop greens.

5. In a blender or food processor, whisk vinegar, sour cream, remaining 1 cup strawberries, and strawberry preserves for 1 minute. Drizzle dressing over salad, and stir until well incorporated.

Summer Strawberry Gazpacho

Adapted from the recipe by Edwina Gadsby

Yield: 6 servings

1 qt. fresh, ripe California strawberries, halved	2 cups celery, diced
½ cup fresh orange juice	¼ cup chopped fresh mint
¼ cup fresh lime juice	1 cup strawberry yogurt
1 sweet onion (such as Walla Walla or Maui), coarsely chopped	Strawberry slices
	Fresh mint sprigs
2 cucumbers, peeled, seeded, and diced	

1. In a food processor or blender, combine halved strawberries, orange juice, lime juice, onion, cucumbers, celery, and chopped mint. Process until still chunky, but do not purée completely. Pour into a large bowl, and whisk in yogurt. Chill at least 30 minutes before serving.

2. Serve gazpacho in chilled bowls garnished with strawberry slices and fresh mint sprigs.

Caribbean Salmon Steaks with Strawberry Salsa

Adapted from the recipe by Patricia Schroedl

Yield: 4 servings

2 cups ripe, fresh California strawberries, chopped

1 cup fresh pineapple, chopped

1 jalapeño pepper, seeded and finely chopped

1 TB. green onions, sliced

1 TB. fresh cilantro, chopped

3 TB. rum

½ tsp. red pepper flakes, crushed

½ tsp. salt

½ cup pineapple juice

¼ cup high-quality strawberry preserves

1 TB. fresh lime juice

1 TB. olive oil

4 (6- to 8-oz.) wild-caught salmon steaks, cut 1-in. thick

Fresh whole strawberry fans

Lime zest curls

Cilantro sprigs

Individual pineapple top leaves

Green onion brushes

1. In a medium bowl, combine strawberries, pineapple, jalapeño pepper, green onions, chopped cilantro, 1 tablespoon rum, ¼ teaspoon red pepper flakes, and ¼ teaspoon salt. Mix well and set aside.

2. In a small saucepan, combine pineapple juice and strawberry preserves over low heat. Heat just until preserves are melted, stirring constantly. Remove from heat, stir in remaining 2 tablespoons rum, lime juice, olive oil, remaining ¼ teaspoon red pepper flakes, and remaining ¼ teaspoon salt. Pour into shallow dish and let cool. Add salmon steaks, turning to coat. Let stand 15 to 20 minutes, turning occasionally.

3. Preheat the broiler. Spray the broiler pan with nonstick cooking spray.

4. Remove salmon steaks from marinade, discarding marinade. Place salmon steaks on the broiler pan, and broil 4 to 6 inches from the heat for 5 minutes. Turn salmon, and broil an additional 3 to 7 minutes or until fish flakes easily with a fork. Stir salsa, and serve over salmon. Garnish with strawberry fans, lime zest curls, cilantro sprigs, pineapple leaves, and green onion brushes.

Strawberry-Marinated Chicken Kabobs

Adapted from the recipe by Darci Gilbert

Yield: 10 to 12 skewers

2 cups fresh, ripe California strawberries

1 TB. butter

¼ cup seasoned rice vinegar

3 TB. olive oil

½ tsp. fresh mint, minced

½ tsp. dried thyme

½ tsp. dried rosemary

4 chicken breast halves, skinned, boned, and cut into ½-in.-wide strips

10 to 12 (8-in.) skewers (soaked in water for at least 30 minutes if using wood/bamboo skewers)

2½ cups pineapple chunks, drained

1 large or 2 small green peppers, seeded and cut into 1-in. squares

12 fresh whole strawberries with stems

Fresh mint leaves

1. In a medium saucepan over medium heat, sauté 2 cups strawberries with butter until berries are softened. Remove from heat, and add to a blender or food processor. Add vinegar, olive oil, mint, thyme, and rosemary, and purée until smooth. Chill marinade until cold.

2. Place chicken strips in a shallow glass dish, and pour cold marinade over top, turning chicken to coat completely. Cover and marinate in the refrigerator 3 or 4 hours or overnight.

3. Preheat the broiler or an outdoor grill.

4. Drain chicken and reserve marinade. Thread each chicken strip back and forth on a bamboo skewer, alternating with pineapple chunks and green pepper squares. Place skewers under the broiler or on grill, and brush with reserved marinade. Cook until chicken is tender.

5. Top each skewer with a whole strawberry, garnish serving platter with fresh mint leaves, and serve hot.

NATIONAL CHERRY FESTIVAL

Traverse City, Michigan
July
1-800-968-3380
www.cherryfestival.org

Founded in 1926, the goal of the National Cherry Festival is to celebrate and promote its marvelous cherries. Thanks to the state of Michigan and the National Cherry Festival, fruit connoisseurs around the county have the opportunity to learn about the little red fruit that's won its place at the table in just about every American home.

Without question, the extraordinary history of the cherry is quite remarkable, having pleased such historical palates as Roman emperors, Greek warriors, and Chinese noblemen. In the 1600s, cherries were shipped across the vast seas and were eventually introduced to the early American settlers. During the mid-1800s, modern cherry production began to emerge. Peter Dougherty, a Presbyterian missionary living in northern Michigan, began planting cherry trees in 1852 on Old Mission Peninsula (near Traverse City). Much to the surprise of the other farmers and Native Americans who lived in the area, Dougherty's cherry trees flourished, and soon other residents of the area planted cherry trees as well.

The first commercial cherry orchards in Michigan were planted in 1893 near the site of Dougherty's original plantings. By the early 1900s, the cherry industry was firmly established in the state. Currently, the United States produces more than 650 million pounds of tart and sweet cherries a year. Michigan grows approximately 75 percent of the tart cherry crop in the United States, or about 250 million pounds.

Feeling a need to promote its star fruit, Michigan pioneered the first official cherry festival in 1926. Today, the National Cherry Festival is stronger than ever, attracting more than 500,000 visitors over 8 fun-filled days. For those seeing a true cherry experience, the festival offers 150 events and activities—85 percent of events free of charge.

Children will enjoy turtle races, pet shows, fishing contests, sand sculptures, junior arts and crafts, prince and princess programs, children's parade, and a very entertaining cherry pie eating contest. For adults who would like to feel like a kid again and sink their teeth into a slice of cherry pie, there is an Adult Cherry Pie Eating Contest. The first one to finish their slice is the winner. Adults and children can also participate in a less messy competition. The Cherry Pit Spit Contest is a fun event offering daily prizes for those who can spit a cherry pit the farthest.

(National Cherry Festival)

Cherry Scones

Adapted from the recipe by the National Cherry Festival

Yield: 8 scones

3½ cups all-purpose flour

¼ cup sugar

1 TB. baking powder

½ tsp. salt

1½ cups heavy cream, plus more as necessary

½ cup honey

Zest of 1 orange

½ cup dried cherries

Coarse sugar

---

1. Preheat the oven to 425°F. Grease a baking sheet.

2. In a mixing bowl, combine flour, sugar, baking powder, and salt. Add cream, honey, and orange zest. Fold in dried cherries. Mix until a smooth dough forms. Do not overmix.

3. Divide dough in ½ and form each ½ into rounds. Slightly flatten each round and cut into 8 equal pieces. Brush with additional cream, and sprinkle with course sugar.

4. Bake for 10 to 12 minutes on the prepared baking sheet.

Cherry Hearth Bread

Adapted from the recipe by the National Cherry Festival

Yield: 2 loaves

1 cup buttermilk	5 cups bread flour
2 cups water	2 cups whole-wheat flour
2 cups apple cider or juice	2 tsp. cinnamon
3 cups honey	1 cup cherries, dried and chopped
2 TB. yeast	1 cup walnuts, chopped
2 TB. salt	

1. In a large bowl, combine buttermilk, water, and apple cider. Add honey and yeast, and stir until combined. Let dough set until yeast has bloomed, about 15 minutes.

2. Add salt, bread flour, whole-wheat flour, cinnamon, cherries, and walnuts, and stir until a stiff dough forms.

3. Turn dough onto a lightly floured board, and knead for 8 to 10 minutes.

4. Return dough to the bowl, and set in a warm place to rise until double in volume, about 1 hour.

5. Punch down and divide into 2 pieces. Round into balls and let rise until almost double.

6. Place each ball on a greased baking sheet and bake in a preheated 375°F oven for 25 to 30 minutes or until golden brown.

Chicken, Cherry, and Wild Rice Salad

Adapted from the recipe by the National Cherry Festival

Yield: 4 servings

¼ cup olive oil	1 (6-oz.) pkg. long grain and wild rice mix
2 TB. soy sauce	2 cups cubed cooked chicken
3 TB. lemon juice	
1½ tsp. ground ginger	1 cup snow pea pods, cut crosswise in ½ and cooked
⅛ tsp. black pepper	½ cup dried tart cherries

1. Combine olive oil, soy sauce, lemon juice, ginger, and pepper. Mix dressing well.

2. Prepare rice according to package directions. Let cooked rice cool for about 15 minutes.

3. Combine cooked chicken, cooked snow peas, and cherries. Pour dressing over chicken mixture, and mix well. Stir cooled rice into chicken mixture. Refrigerate, covered, at least 1 hour before serving.

Cherry-Marinated Flank Steak

Adapted from the recipe by the National Cherry Festival

Yield: 4 servings

2 cups molasses	1 TB. fresh cracked black pepper
1 cup red wine	1 tsp. fresh thyme
3 cups cherry juice concentrate	1 (2- or 3-lb.) flank steak
4 cloves garlic, smashed	Salt
3 cups balsamic vinegar	Pepper

1. In a mixing bowl, combine molasses, red wine, cherry juice, garlic, balsamic vinegar, black pepper, and thyme.

2. Place steak in a large shallow baking dish. Pour marinade over steak and turn to coat. Cover and let marinate in the refrigerator at least 4 hours or overnight.

3. Heat an outdoor grill over high heat. Remove steak from marinade, and season with salt and pepper. Grill for 4 minutes on each side for medium-rare.

Cherry Pulled Pork

Adapted from the recipe by the National Cherry Festival

Barbecue Rub:	Cherry Basting Sauce:	Cherry Vinegar Sauce:
1 TB. brown sugar	1 cup cider vinegar	2 cups cider vinegar
¼ cup paprika	½ cup cherry juice concentrate	½ cup cherry juice concentrate
1 tsp. black pepper	1 TB. onion powder	¼ cup ketchup
4 TB. salt	1 TB. granulated garlic	2 TB. brown sugar
2 tsp. garlic powder	1 TB. Tabasco sauce	1 tsp. black pepper
2 tsp. onion powder	1 TB. salt	1 TB. salt
2 tsp. celery seed	1 TB. brown sugar	1 TB. Tabasco sauce
1 tsp. cayenne	1 tsp. black pepper	1 (5- to 7-lb.) pork butt roast

1. Prepare Barbecue Rub: combine brown sugar, paprika, black pepper, salt, garlic powder, onion powder, celery seed, and cayenne. Store rub in an airtight container.

2. Prepare Cherry Basting Sauce: combine cider vinegar, cherry juice concentrate, onion powder, granulated garlic, Tabasco sauce, salt, brown sugar, and black pepper. Blend well, store in a glass jar, and use as needed.

3. Prepare Cherry Vinegar Sauce: combine cider vinegar, cherry juice concentrate, ketchup, brown sugar, black pepper, salt, and Tabasco sauce. Blend well, store in a glass jar, and use as needed.

4. Sprinkle rub on pork shoulder and press in to coat thoroughly. Cook pork immediately, or marinate, refrigerated, for up to 24 hours.

5. Preheat an outdoor grill to high heat.

6. Create a smoking pouch by adding 1 cup wet and dry wood chips in a foil pouch, punching holes in both sides. Place the pouch on the preheated grill, and cook on high until you see smoke. Reduce heat to low.

7. Add pork to the grill and cook for 4 to 6 hours or until pork is very tender; the internal temperature should be 195°F. Baste pork intermittently with Cherry Basting Sauce.

8. When pork is finished cooking, remove it from the grill and pull apart while it's hot. Mix pork with enough Cherry Vinegar Sauce until meat is moist.

9. To serve, place some pulled pork on a toasted bun and top with coleslaw.

MORTON PUMPKIN FESTIVAL

Morton, Illinois
September
1-888-765-6588
www.pumpkincapital.com

Morton, Illinois, is the Pumpkin Capital of the World. Home of Nestlé/Libby's pumpkin packing plant, 80 percent of the world's canned pumpkin is processed here. And celebrating the beginning of the pumpkin canning season every September, the town of Morton turns to their fabulous pumpkin festival, which has been going strong for more than 40 years.

From the opening day ceremonies to the giant festival parade, the Morton Pumpkin Festival amuses visitors of all ages with family-style entertainment, carnival rides, foot races, food and merchant tents, craft shows, a parade, and plenty of pumpkins.

Plenty of delicious pumpkin food is also available. Butterfly pork chops and pumpkin pie are the specialties, along with pumpkin ice cream, pumpkin pancakes, and pumpkin fudge. The Pumpkin Cookery contest, sponsored by Nestlé/Libby's, features award-winning recipes for cakes, cookies, breads, pies, desserts, main dishes, appetizers, soups, and other savory items. The main rule is that at least 1 cup of Libby's 100% Pure Pumpkin is incorporated into each submitted recipe.

Can't get enough pumpkin at the festival? Then check out the festival's Pumpkin Weigh-In. No matter where you live, if you have a big, beautiful pumpkin growing you may enter it in the Pumpkin Festival Open Contest. There's also a competition for the mature orange pumpkin weighing exactly 39 pounds. After the pumpkin weigh-ins, a themed parade commences, where pumpkin winners escort their trophies and prize pumpkins on a float.

But the highlight of the festival is the famous Punkin Chuckin' Contest. Here, great machines hurl pumpkins thousands of feet into the air. Two of Morton's most famous chuckin' machines—which have appeared on the *Late Show with David Letterman*—are the Q36 Pumpkin Modulator and the Acme Catapult. The Q36 established a Guinness World Record in 1998 with a chuck of 4,491 feet, and in 2001, a pumpkin was flung 4,860 feet, which is still the world record.

(Morton Pumpkin Festival)

Pumpkin Ribbon Bread

Adapted from the recipe by Sara Schlink

6 oz. cream cheese	2 egg whites
1½ cups sugar	1 TB. canola oil
1⅔ cups plus 1 TB. flour	1 tsp. baking soda
1½ tsp. cinnamon	½ tsp. salt
1 cup Libby's 100% Pure Pumpkin	½ tsp. cloves
½ cup unsweetened applesauce	⅓ cup chopped walnuts (optional)
1 egg	

1. Preheat the oven to 350°F. Grease a 8½×4½×2¾-inch loaf pan.

2. In a small bowl, combine cream cheese, ¼ cup sugar, 1 tablespoon flour, and 1 teaspoon cinnamon. Set aside.

3. In a mixing bowl, beat pumpkin, applesauce, egg, egg whites, and oil.

4. In a separate bowl, combine remaining 1⅔ cups flour, remaining 1¼ cups sugar, baking soda, salt, remaining ½ teaspoon cinnamon, and cloves, and add to pumpkin mixture. Stir in nuts (if using).

5. Spread ½ batter in the prepared pan, and spread with cream cheese filling mixture. Top with remaining batter.

6. Bake for 50 minutes or until a toothpick inserted into the center comes out clean.

Pumpkin Hummus

Adapted from the recipe by Michelle Parker

Yield: 15 to 20 servings

2 (15-oz.) cans garbanzo beans, drained	Juice of 1 lemon
1 cup Libby's 100% Pure Pumpkin	1½ cup garlic-infused extra-virgin olive oil*
2 TB. smooth peanut butter	
1½ TB. brown sugar	2 TB. kosher salt or to taste
2 TB. cumin	1 tsp. paprika or to taste
2 cloves garlic, crushed	1 pkg. whole-wheat pita bread
	Pine nuts, lightly toasted

1. In a food processor, purée garbanzo beans, pumpkin, peanut butter, brown sugar, cumin, garlic, lemon juice, and enough olive oil to make a paste of dip consistency. Add kosher salt to taste, and purée until smooth.

2. Spread hummus onto a round platter. Drizzle with additional olive oil, and sprinkle with paprika to taste.

3. Lightly toast pita bread. Cut each piece into 8 wedges, and place around hummus. Sprinkle pine nuts over the top, and serve immediately.

*To make garlic-infused olive oil, add 9 garlic cloves, halved lengthwise, to 1½ cups olive oil and cook for 30 to 40 minutes in a saucepan over the gentlest heat possible. Remove garlic and let cool before using.

Chicken and Pumpkin Salad Wraps

Adapted from the recipe by Dianna Wara

Yield: 4 servings

1½ lb. boneless, skinless chicken	½ tsp. garlic powder
3 cups 100 percent grape juice	1 TB. yellow mustard
⅓ cup cooked and crumbled bacon	½ tsp. salt
⅓ cup chopped pecans	¼ tsp. black pepper
½ cup mayonnaise	½ cup shredded Romano cheese
1 (4-oz.) pkg. sour cream	30 red seedless grapes, quartered
1 cup Libby's 100% Pure Pumpkin	4 slices flat or pita bread
2 TB. fresh basil, chopped	1 cup shredded lettuce
½ tsp. dehydrated minced onion	

1. Add chicken and grape juice to a Dutch oven. Add enough water to just cover chicken. Cook on high until boiling. Reduce heat, cover, and let simmer until chicken is no longer pink in the center.

2. While chicken is cooking, mix bacon, pecans, mayonnaise, sour cream, pumpkin, basil, onion, garlic powder, mustard, salt, pepper, and cheese in a large bowl. Cover and refrigerate.

3. When chicken is fully cooked, drain well. Place chicken on a cutting board, and using forks, flake chicken into small, bite-size pieces. Add chicken to salad mixture bowl. Add grapes and mix well. Refrigerate chicken salad until ready to serve.

4. Prior to serving, evenly divide chicken salad among 4 pieces of flat or pita bread. Spread salad from end to end, top with shredded lettuce, and roll from short end to short end. Cut in ½ and serve.

Pumpkin Caramels

Adapted from the recipe by Sally Zwanzig

Yield: 15 to 20 servings

---

3 cups sugar

3 cups white corn syrup

½ cup butter

2 cups whipping cream

1 cup Libby's 100% Pure Pumpkin

1 (14-oz.) can Eagle Brand condensed milk

¾ tsp. salt

2 tsp. vanilla extract

---

1. Grease two 9×13 pans.

2. In a medium saucepan, bring sugar, corn syrup, and butter to a boil. Add 1 cup whipping cream, and bring to boil until a candy thermometer reads 240°F. Add remaining 1 cup whipping cream and bring back to 240°F. Add pumpkin and condensed milk. Bring back to 240°F. Remove from heat, and add salt and vanilla extract.

3. Pour mixture into prepared pans. Let cool.

4. When cool, cut candies and wrap in wax paper.

Variation: Add 1½ cups broken pecans and 1½ teaspoon pumpkin pie spice when adding salt and vanilla extract.

Pumpkin Fudge

Adapted from the recipe by Mrs. Sherry Hughbanks

Yield: Makes about 36 squares

1 cup milk	½ tsp. cinnamon
3 cups granulated sugar	½ tsp. allspice
3 TB. light corn syrup	4 TB. butter
½ cup Libby's 100% Pure Pumpkin	1 tsp. vanilla extract
Dash salt	

1. In a medium saucepan, combine milk, sugar, corn syrup, pumpkin, and salt. Bring to a boil over high heat, stirring constantly. Reduce heat to medium and continue boiling. Do not stir. When mixture registers 232°F on candy thermometer, or forms a soft ball when dropped into cold water, remove pan from heat.

2. Stir in cinnamon, allspice, butter, and vanilla extract. Allow to cool.

3. When cool, beat until thick and mixture loses its gloss. Quickly pour into a buttered 8-inch pan. Cut into squares when firm.

BLACK WALNUT FESTIVAL

Spenser, West Virginia
October
304-927-5616
www.wvblackwalnutfestival.org

For more than 50 years, the West Virginia Black Walnut Festival in Spenser has grown from a 1-day event to a 4-day celebration, attracting thousands of visitors from across the United States. The Black Walnut Festival is one of West Virginia's best-attended festivals, and continues to offer a plethora of activities for everyone.

In 1954, local farmer Henry Young felt he struck gold when he sold 2 million pounds of black walnuts. Young's transaction gave a member of the Little Kanawha Regional Council the idea of developing black walnuts into a cash crop. One year later, the first Black Walnut Festival was held. At the end of the day, festival organizers realized a 1-day celebration would not be enough, and so the festival began to grow.

Today, the Black Walnut Festival kicks off with a pancake breakfast, followed by chainsaw artists, antique shows, live music performances, a carnival, firemen's competition, livestock sale, long-distance nut run, car show, Kid's Day Parade, a Black Walnut Bake-Off, and food concessions selling baked goods and cookbooks featuring West Virginia's famous black walnuts.

The black walnut is prized by bakeries and candy makers for its rich, robust flavor, which cannot be found in regular store-bought walnuts. Black walnuts are also low in saturated fats; have no cholesterol; and contain iron, minerals, and fiber.

Before eating, black walnuts should be cured in a dry place for at least 2 weeks. Before cracking, the unshelled nuts may be soaked in hot water for 24 hours to soften, but with a proper cracker, this shouldn't be necessary.

Black Walnut Bread

Adapted from the recipe by Marlene Grady

Yield: 1 loaf

2½ cups all-purpose flour	3 TB. salad oil
1 cup sugar	1¼ cups whole milk
3½ tsp. baking powder	1 egg
1 tsp. salt	1 cup finely chopped West Virginia black walnuts

1. Preheat the oven 350°F. Grease and flour a 9×5×3-inch loaf pan.

2. In a large mixing bowl, combine flour, sugar, baking powder, salt, oil, milk, and egg. Beat with a mixer on medium speed for 30 seconds, scrapping the sides and the bottom of the bowl constantly.

3. Stir in walnuts. Pour batter into the prepared pan.

4. Bake for 55 to 65 minutes or until a toothpick inserted in the center comes out clean. Remove bread from the pan and cool thoroughly before slicing.

West Virginia Black Walnut Surprise

Adapted from the recipe by Debbie Cottrell

---

2 cups shredded squash

2 cups sugar

1 cup oil

3 eggs

3 cups all-purpose flour

¾ cup West Virginia black walnuts

1 tsp. salt

1 tsp. baking powder

1 tsp. baking soda

2 tsp. vanilla extract

1 (3.4-oz.) box lemon instant pudding

¼ cup raisins

4 TB. butter or margarine, softened

3 cups confectioners' sugar

2 TB. lemon juice

1 tsp. lemon extract

Few grains salt

1 or 2 TB. cold water

---

1. Preheat the oven to 325°F.

2. In a large mixing bowl, combine shredded squash, sugar, oil, eggs, flour, walnuts, 1 teaspoon salt, baking powder, baking soda, vanilla extract, pudding, and raisins. Pour batter into a cake mold and bake for 30 minutes.

3. Cream butter, and add confectioners' sugar gradually, creaming thoroughly. Beat in lemon juice, lemon extract, salt, and enough water to make frosting spreading consistency.

4. Spread lemon butter frosting on cool cake.

Black Walnut Harvest Pie

Adapted from the recipe by Ruby Black

Yield: 1 pie

⅓ cup Crisco	3 eggs
¼ tsp. salt	¼ tsp. salt
1 cup sifted flour	1 cup sugar
3 TB. water	1 tsp. vanilla extract
½ tsp. vinegar	2 TB. butter
½ cup heavy cream	1½ cups chopped West Virginia black walnuts
½ cup dark corn syrup	

1. Preheat the oven to 400°F.

2. In a mixing bowl, combine Crisco, salt, and ½ cup flour. Add water, vinegar, and remaining ½ cup flour, and mix until the sides of the bowl are clean. Roll out piecrust dough until it fits a 9-inch pie pan.

3. In another bowl, combine cream, corn syrup, eggs, salt, sugar, vanilla extract, and butter. Add walnuts and stir to combine. Pour batter into unbaked 9-inch piecrust.

4. Bake pie for 10 minutes. Reduce heat to 350°F and bake an additional 25 minutes.

Black Walnut Pinwheels

Adapted from the recipe by Robert Raines

Yield: 7 to 8 dozen

---

1 cup shortening	2 TB. milk
3⅓ cups brown sugar	⅔ cup butter or margarine
2 eggs, unbeaten	½ cup cream
1½ tsp. salt	1 tsp. black walnut flavoring
3⅓ cups all-purpose flour	2 cups finely ground West Virginia black walnuts
1½ tsp. baking soda	

---

1. In a mixing bowl, combine shortening, 2 cups brown sugar, and eggs. Cream well. Add salt, flour, baking soda, and milk. Stir well until blended, and chill.

2. Prepare filling. In a medium saucepan, combine butter, remaining 1⅓ cups brown sugar, cream, black walnut flavoring, and ground walnuts. Cook over medium-high heat until brown and bubbly. Cool.

3. Remove chilled dough from the refrigerator, and roll out dough to ¼ inch thick. Spread with filling, and roll up like a jelly roll. Chill.

4. Slice chilled dough into ¼-inch slices. Bake on an ungreased cookie sheet at 375°F for 8 to 10 minutes.

Black Walnut Delights

Adapted from the recipe by June Russell

1⅓ cups sugar

⅔ cup nondairy liquid coffee creamer

½ cup butter or margarine

⅛ tsp. salt

2 cups miniature marshmallows

½ lb. white chocolate, finely chopped

1 tsp. vanilla extract

1 lb. milk chocolate, finely chopped

¼ cup black walnuts, chopped

1. Butter an 8-inch square pan.

2. In a medium saucepan, combine sugar, creamer, butter, and salt. Cook over medium heat, without stirring, until mixture reaches 140°F on a candy thermometer.

3. Remove from heat and add marshmallows, white chocolate, black walnuts, and vanilla extract, stirring until marshmallows melt.

4. Pour into the prepared square pan. Cool.

5. Roll into balls, place on a cookie sheet, and chill.

6. Bring water to a boil in a double boiler (water should not touch top part of double boiler, as it will burn chocolate) and remove from heat.

7. Add milk chocolate in the top part of a double boiler and melt. Stir to help with melting process.

8. Dip each ball into milk chocolate, place on cookie sheet, and chill.

NATIONAL PEANUT FESTIVAL

Dothan, Alabama
November
866-277-3962
www.nationalpeanutfestival.com

Sixty-five percent of all the peanuts grown in the United States are grown within a 100-mile radius of Dothan, Alabama. Hence, Dothan is known as the "Peanut Capital of the World" and is home to the National Peanut Festival—the nation's largest peanut festival—honoring peanut growers and celebrating harvest season.

The festival was inaugurated in 1938 on a near-freezing November day in Dothan. The 3-day event included a pageant, parade, historical play, and grand ball. The honored guest speaker was Dr. George Washington Carver, who gained international fame with his development of more than 300 products from the peanut. The famed peanut festival was held every year until 1942. During the years of World War II the festival was postponed, but in 1947, the Jaycees presented the first post-war festival, and it has continued every year since.

By 1952, the National Peanut Festival had expanded to such an enormous size, the Chamber of Commerce didn't have the time to sponsor and oversee the event. After another overwhelming turnout at the 1953 National Peanut Festival, the Chamber agreed that a carnival should be included to help finance the annual event.

Today, the National Peanut Festival has grown from a 3-day event in the late 1930s to a 10-day event at the 150-acre fairgrounds with attendance in excess of 163,000 visitors. More than 500 volunteers devote countless hours to the festival to ensure its success. The peanut, peanut growers, and local agriculture industries are to be commended for their dedication and for giving the area a reason for celebrating such an important economic product.

(National Peanut Festival)

Peanut Crackers

Adapted from the recipe by Charlotte Fulgham

---

40 saltine or graham crackers

1 cup (2 sticks) butter or margarine

1 cup sugar

1½ cups roasted peanuts, chopped

½ tsp. vanilla extract

---

1. Preheat the oven to 350°F.

2. Arrange saltine crackers in a single layer on a cookie sheet.

3. In a medium saucepan, bring butter, sugar, and peanuts to a boil. Boil for 3 minutes, stirring often. Add vanilla extract and mix well.

4. Spoon peanuts in the center of each cracker. Pour remaining sauce over each cracker, being sure to cover top of each one.

5. Bake for 12 minutes. With a spatula, immediately remove crackers to a wire rack to cool. Store in airtight container.

Nutter Butter Cheesecake Truffles

Adapted from the recipe by Traci Mitchell

Yield: About 42 truffles

---

1 (16-oz.) pkg. Nutter Butter cookies

1 (8-oz.) pkg. cream cheese, softened

1 pkg. white chocolate confectioners' coating

1 tsp. LorAnn Cheesecake Flavoring (optional)

---

1. Crush 5 cookies to fine crumbs in a food processor. Set aside. Crush remaining cookies to fine crumbs, and place in a medium bowl. Add cream cheese, and mix until well blended.

2. Roll cookie mixture into 1-inch balls. Place on a parchment-lined baking sheet. Refrigerate until firm, about 1 hour.

3. Melt white chocolate candy coating and cheesecake flavoring (if using; find this in most cake and candy supply stores) according to package directions.

4. Dip cookie balls into chocolate, and place on a waxed paper–lined baking sheet. Sprinkle with reserved cookie crumbs. Store truffles covered in refrigerator.

Nutter Butter Peanut Butter Pie

Adapted from the recipe by Melisa Huddleston

Yield: 1 pie

1 (16-oz.) pkg. Nutter Butter cookies, crushed	1 cup peanut butter
	½ cup confectioners' sugar
1 TB. sugar	1 (16-oz.) tub Cool Whip
6 TB. butter, melted	1 (8-oz.) pkg. cream cheese
1 cup chocolate morsels	8 Nutter Butter cookies, crushed

1. In a pie plate, mix package of cookie crumbs, sugar, and melted butter, and spread out mixture to form crust. Refrigerate for 1 hour.

2. Melt chocolate morsels and pour over crust. Chill for about 15 minutes.

3. In a mixing bowl, combine peanut butter, confectioners' sugar, Cool Whip, cream cheese, and 8 crushed cookies. Pour filling on top of chocolate-coated crust, and chill ½ hour or until serving time.

4. Before serving, top with extra Cool Whip and decorate to your liking.

Carmel Peanut Pie

Adapted from the recipe by Mavis Slay

Yield: 2 pies

2 (9-in.) pie shells	1 (8-oz.) pkg. cream cheese
½ cup butter	1 (14-oz.) can condensed milk
1 cup coconut	1 (16-oz.) tub Cool Whip
1 cup peanuts	1 (12-oz.) pkg. caramel ice cream topping

1. Bake pie shells according to package directions and cool.

2. Melt butter. Combine ¼ cup with coconut and ¼ cup with peanuts in separate bowls. Spread in a single layer on two baking sheets and toast in a 400°F oven until golden brown. Cool.

3. In a mixing bowl, combine cream cheese and condensed milk, and beat until smooth. Fold in Cool Whip.

4. Layer ¼ of cream cheese mixture in each pie shell. Sprinkle with ¼ of peanuts and ¼ of coconut.

5. Microwave caramel ice cream topping in the jar without the lid for 30 to 45 seconds and top pies by drizzling over peanuts and coconut.

6. Freeze pies until 15 to 20 minutes before serving.

Pink Passion
Triple Peanut Butter Cake

Adapted from the recipe by Mary Rogers Davis

Yield: 1 cake

Cake:	Icing:
½ cup peanut butter	½ cup peanut butter
⅓ cup peanut oil	⅓ cup Crisco shortening (butter flavor)
2 sticks unsalted butter	8 oz. cream cheese
1 cup whipping cream	1 tsp. McCormick Imitation Vanilla Flavor
6 jumbo eggs	5 cups confectioners' sugar
1½ tsp. imitation vanilla extract	⅓ cup whipping cream, plus 2 TB. if too thick
2 tsp. McCormick Imitation Butter Flavor	
2 cups sugar	1 tsp. red food coloring
3 cups flour	1 tsp. strawberry jam
2 tsp. baking powder	1 cup chopped peanuts (unsalted, dry roasted, or toffee covered)
¼ tsp. salt	1 whole strawberry

1. Preheat the oven to 325°F.

2. Prepare cake: in a mixing bowl, combine peanut butter, peanut oil, and butter until smooth. Add whipping cream, eggs, vanilla extract, McCormick Imitation Butter Flavor, and sugar. Beat until smooth, about 2 minutes. Add flour, baking powder, and salt, and mix until smooth, about 2 minutes.

3. Spray 2 (10-inch) pie pans with cooking spray and line with waxed paper. Divide batter between the 2 pans. Bake for 40 to 45 minutes or until done.

4. Prepare icing: in a mixing bowl, combine peanut butter, Crisco, and cream cheese until smooth. Add McCormick Imitation Vanilla Flavor, confectioners' sugar, and whipping cream, and blend until smooth.

5. Remove 1½ cup icing to a separate bowl and add food coloring and strawberry jam. Blend with a spoon until smooth and set aside.

6. Place ½ of pink icing in the center of first layer, and cover remaining layer with peanut butter frosting. Place top layer on cake, and secure with 2 paper candy sticks pushed down on opposite sides of cake. Ice top layer center with pink icing, and ice remaining cake with peanut butter frosting.

7. Garnish cake with peanuts around the bottom of cake and top with strawberry.

CALIFORNIA AVOCADO FESTIVAL

Carpinteria, California
October
805-684-5479 (Carpinteria Valley Chamber of Commerce)
www.avofest.com

Every year, Carpinteria, California, entertains more than 140,000 visitors from every part of the globe during its California Avocado Festival, the largest free festival on the central coast. Recently, the festival received national recognition on the Food Network as part of their *Great American Festivals* program.

The idea for a California avocado festival began in 1984 when a brainstorming meeting was called to create an ongoing weekend event that would promote Carpinteria as a southern California weekend getaway destination and boost the local economy. But why avocados? Currently, California is the leading producer of domestic avocados and home to about 90 percent of the nation's crop. Seven varieties of avocados are grown commercially in California, with the Hass the most popular, accounting for approximately 95 percent of the total crop volume. Most California avocados are harvested on 60,000 acres between San Luis Obispo and the Mexican border, with Carpinteria being a major contributor. California avocados, also known as Alligator Pears because of their pearlike shape and green skin, are grown year-round. A single California avocado tree can produce up to 200 pounds of fresh fruit each year—approximately 500 pieces—although most average around 60 pounds, or 150 pieces of fruit.

Today, the California Avocado Festival has evolved into one of the largest in California, with 3 days of food, music, and family fun. Recently, the festival expanded to include 70 arts-and-crafts venues and food demonstrations with local chefs, along with 30 fun-filled booths and more than 30 commercial vendors. There's even a Largest Avocado Contest, based purely on weight, and a Best Guacamole Contest to celebrate the famous green fruit. Each year, judges sample more than 30 guacamole recipes and award prizes based on presentation, taste, and originality.

(California Avocado Festival)

Mexi-Fest Guacamole

Adapted from the recipe by Angelina Garcia

Yield: Approximately 1 quart

10 yellow chilies, finely diced	1 bunch cilantro, finely cut
8 tomatoes, diced	⅓ cup fresh lemon juice
3 sweet onions, diced	6 to 8 fresh, ripe avocados, diced

1. In a large mixing bowl, combine yellow chilies, tomatoes, onions, cilantro, and lemon juice.

2. Fold in avocados.

Home-Grown Guacamole

Adapted from the recipe by Melissa Fowler

Yield: Approximately 1 quart

3 tomatoes, chopped and seeded	6 Hass avocados, peeled and diced
5 green onions, chopped	Juice of 1 lime
½ sweet onion	Sea salt
1 clove garlic, mashed	Black pepper
½ jalapeño pepper	Seasoning salt
1 (4-oz.) can mild chilies	4 Hass avocados, peeled and chunked
Juice of 1 lemon	

1. In a bowl, fold together tomatoes, green onions, sweet onion, garlic, jalapeño, mild chilies, lemon juice, diced avocados, lime juice, sea salt, black pepper, and seasoning salt. Chill.

2. Blend in chunked avocados just before serving.

"Traditional" Mix Guacamole

Adapted from the recipe by Angelina Garcia

Yield: Approximately 1 quart

2 fresh chili de arbol	2 cups cilantro
2 fresh serrano peppers	4 cloves garlic
1 fresh yellow pepper	Salt
1 fresh jalapeño pepper	1 cup diced red onion
2 or 3 fresh tomatoes	1 cup diced green onion
½ tsp. oregano	6 large avocados, peeled and diced

1. In a large saucepan, boil chili de arbol, serrano peppers, yellow pepper, and jalapeño pepper in water. (You could also roast chilies and mash on stone later.)

2. In another saucepan, boil tomatoes in water.

3. In a blender, combine peppers, tomatoes, oregano, cilantro, and garlic just until grated. Add salt to taste.

4. Add diced red and green onions and stir.

5. Add avocado until desired thickness and richness is reached.

Ahuaca-Hulli Guacamole

Adapted from the recipe by Trish Combs

Yield: Approximately 1 quart

3 medium organic tomatoes	2 tsp. Hawaiian sea salt
Vegetable oil	1 bunch cilantro
Salt and pepper	½ tsp. garlic
6 jalapeño peppers, roasted and peeled	10 Hass avocados
2 habanero peppers, roasted	2 tsp. fresh lemon juice
1 medium yellow onion, diced	

1. Cut tomatoes about ½-inch thick, brush with vegetable oil, season with salt and pepper, and grill over an open flame for about 2 minutes per side.

2. With a large mortar and pestle, grind jalapeño and habanero peppers. Add onion and grind again. Add Hawaiian sea salt, cilantro, garlic, and tomatoes, and stir to combine.

3. Cut avocados in half around pit and twist gently to pull apart. Remove pit. Cube avocado in skin, and gently turn skin inside out and scoop into the mortar. Repeat with all avocados. Finish by folding in lemon juice.

STOCKTON ASPARAGUS FESTIVAL

Stockton, California
April
209-644-3740
www.asparagusfest.com

Welcome to the Stockton Asparagus Festival, voted one of the Best Food Festivals in the West! Get ready to enjoy 3 days of fun and exciting entertainment.

Created in 1988 to honor San Joaquin County's most prestigious agricultural product, the Stockton Asparagus Festival is a multi-event food and entertainment festival for all ages. Attendees to the annual festival are guaranteed to get their fill of asparagus as they choose between the festival's performing stages, Asparagus Alley—the heart of the festival with the best deep-fried asparagus found anywhere, the finest celebrity chef cooking demonstrations, a fabulous beer and wine pavilion, an arts-and-crafts show, and endless exhibits put on by 70 food purveyors and 100 specialty merchandise vendors.

The festival goes through an estimated 40,000 pounds of asparagus every year. And because the asparagus is grown locally, it's the freshest you can get. In fact, much of the asparagus is cut fresh from nearby fields every day of the festival. From the delicious deep-fried asparagus and pasta dishes, to refreshing drinks and more, The Stockton Asparagus Festival offers bushels of endless treats sure to please.

Visitors also come for the highly touted Recipe Contest, which recently made its claim to fame on the Food Network. So long as the recipe contains fresh, frozen, or canned asparagus, all recipes qualify, including appetizers, cookies, cakes, pies, quiches, soups, stews, relishes, salsas, jams, jellies, muffins, and breads.

Over at the World Deep-Fried Asparagus Eating Competition, excitement is always feverish. Not long ago, a petite 105-pound gal won the first-ever Deep-Fried Asparagus Eating Championship by consuming 5.7 pounds of deep-fried asparagus in 10 minutes.

(Stockton Asparagus Festival)

Asparagus Bisque

Adapted from the recipe by the Stockton Asparagus Festival

Yield: 1 gallon

---

8 TB. (1 stick) butter	3 cups cleaned and cooked asparagus, tips and center cuts only, cut into ½-in. pieces
¾ cup flour	
2 qt. whole milk	1 pkg. instant potatoes
1 cup chicken stock (made from bouillon cube)	Sourdough croutons
1 bay leaf	Sour cream
1 tsp. white pepper	Fresh dill weed
1 tsp. salt	

---

1. In a stockpot, melt butter. Add flour, stirring constantly so mixture doesn't burn. Add 1 quart milk slowly, stirring constantly. When combined and thickened, add remaining milk and chicken stock. Add bay leaf, white pepper, and salt. Add asparagus. Cook soup slowly for 1 hour, adding instant potatoes as necessary to thicken.

2. To serve, remove bay leaf and top bisque with sourdough croutons and a spoonful of sour cream. Sprinkle with dill weed.

Asparagus and Shrimp Salad

Adapted from the recipe by the Stockton Asparagus Festival

Yield: 4 servings

1 lb. cooked and peeled salad shrimp	1 tsp. salt
1 lb. asparagus tips, cooked to tender	1 cup mayonnaise
½ cup chopped pimientos	1 TB. horseradish
¼ cup finely chopped parsley	Endive and green lettuce
¼ cup fresh squeezed lemon juice	1 lemon, cut into wedges
½ tsp. white pepper	2 hard-boiled eggs, diced
½ tsp. celery seed	

1. In a bowl, combine shrimp, asparagus, pimientos, parsley, lemon juice, white pepper, celery seed, salt, horseradish, and mayonnaise.

2. Arrange leaves of endive and lettuce on serving plates, and top with shrimp salad. Garnish with lemon wedge, and top with diced egg.

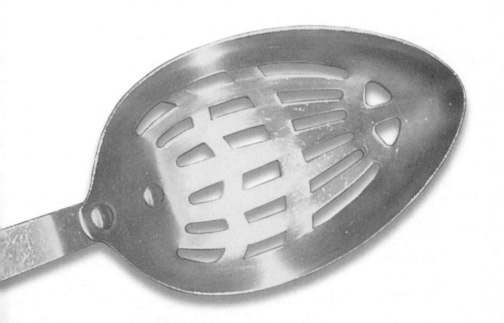

Deep-Fried Asparagus

Adapted from the recipe by the Stockton Asparagus Festival

½ cup cornstarch	½ tsp. baking soda
¾ cup flour	1 tsp. baking powder
1 tsp. salt	2 egg whites
¼ tsp. black pepper	⅔ cup cold flat beer
½ tsp. white pepper	Peanut oil
½ tsp. celery salt	2 cups (3 lb.) raw, whole asparagus, cleaned and cut above white end

1. In a bowl, combine cornstarch, flour, salt, black pepper, white pepper, celery salt, baking soda, baking powder, egg whites, and cold flat beer with a wire whisk until well blended.

2. In a large saucepan, bring 2 inches peanut oil to high-heat (oil should pop and crackle).

3. Dip asparagus individually in the batter and deep fry in peanut oil for 2 minutes or until golden brown.

Asparagus Pasta

Adapted from the recipe by the Stockton Asparagus Festival

16 oz. fusilli pasta

1 cup sliced fresh mushrooms

½ cup chopped green onions

4 cloves garlic, minced

⅓ cup olive oil

½ cup olive wedges

1 cup diced tomatoes (fresh or canned, drained)

2 cups cooked asparagus, tips and center cuts only

1 TB. Italian seasoning

1 TB. salt

1 tsp. pepper

½ cup marsala wine

1½ cups chicken stock

Cornstarch wash (equal amounts of cornstarch and water)

Grated Romano cheese

1. Cook pasta according to package directions.

2. In a large skillet over high heat, sauté mushrooms, green onion, and garlic in olive oil until tender. Add olives and tomatoes, and heat thoroughly. Add cooked asparagus, Italian seasoning, salt, and pepper, stirring constantly. Add marsala wine to flash point (the lowest temperature at which wine can form an ignitable mixture in air) and then add chicken stock. Add cornstarch wash to thicken as necessary.

3. Pour sauce over cooked pasta, mix, sprinkle with grated Romano cheese, and serve hot.

IDAHO–EASTERN OREGON ONION FESTIVAL

Ontario, Oregon
August
541-889-8012 (Ontario Chamber of Commerce)
www.onionfestival.com

Idaho's and Eastern Oregon's onion-growing region is the largest in the United States. Approximately 21,000 acres of onions are planted every year during March and April, with harvest taking place in August and continuing until October. Yellow, red, and white onions are the popular varieties grown in this region, with yellow onions accounting for 90 percent of the harvest. Onions harvested in Idaho and Eastern Oregon account for 23 percent of the bulb onions consumed annually in the United States. Paying tribute to the 350 growers and 36 shippers of Idaho–Eastern Oregon, an onion festival was organized. Today, that festival educates and entertains the public with—what else?—onions.

One of the highlights of the annual Idaho–Eastern Oregon Onion Festival is the Onion Cooking Contest. At this event, eager cooks prepare an assortment of appetizers, salads, relishes, main dishes, and breads, all containing onions, which is believed to be one of the earliest wild plants to be cultivated. In fact, the onion was a well-loved food in the ancient world, and to show their appreciation, artists painted the renowned vegetable on Egypt's pyramids.

Another popular event at the festival is the Onion Decorating Contest. The decoration can be any arrangement from a garden bouquet to an onion doll to an animal figurine.

The devoted onion farmers of the region are always honored at the Big Onion Contest, where farmers can bring in their largest onions for the chance to win prize money and recognition among fellow growers.

For nonfarmers who may find themselves producing the largest onion, a Gardener Big Onion Contest is open to the public.

Of course, a food festival couldn't be complete without an eating contest, and the Idaho–Eastern Oregon Onion Festival is no exception. The festival's Onion Ring Eating Contest is a fun event that consists of three-person relay teams eating onion rings in a timed race. *Bon appétit.*

(Idaho–Eastern Oregon Onion Festival)

Onion Herb Bread

Adapted from the recipe by the Idaho–Eastern Oregon Onion Committee

Yield: 1 loaf

1½ cups yellow onion, finely chopped	1 cup milk
2 TB. butter or margarine	1 tsp. basil
3 cups dry buttermilk baking mix	1 tsp. dill weed
1 egg	

1. Preheat the oven to 350°F. Grease a 9×5 loaf pan.

2. In a skillet, sauté onion in butter until tender.

3. In a separate bowl, combine baking mix, egg, and milk. Add basil, dill weed, and cooked onions, and mix until blended. Spoon into the prepared pan. Bake for 55 to 60 minutes.

Hot Onion Pasta Salad

Adapted from the recipe by the Idaho–Eastern Oregon Onion Committee

Yield: 6 servings

8 oz. pasta of your choice	1 tsp. sugar
1 jumbo yellow onion	2 tsp. prepared mustard
4 slices bacon	½ tsp. salt
Salad oil	¼ tsp. pepper
1 clove garlic, minced	Lettuce
3 TB. vinegar	Yellow onion rings
3 TB. water	

1. Cook pasta according to package directions.

2. Peel and finely chop onion to measure 1½ cups.

3. In a skillet, fry bacon until crisp. Remove bacon from the skillet and crumble. Drain and reserve skillet drippings.

4. Measure bacon drippings, adding salad oil if necessary to make 3 tablespoons. Heat drippings, and add chopped onion and garlic. Sauté until onion is translucent.

5. Stir in vinegar, water, sugar, mustard, salt, and pepper, and heat gently.

6. Toss hot dressing with hot cooked pasta, and serve on a bed of lettuce. Garnish with onion rings.

Soy Onion Chicken

Adapted from the recipe by the Idaho–Eastern Oregon Onion Committee

---

Yield: 6 servings

Flour	2 medium (8- to 10-oz.) yellow onions
¼ tsp. ginger (optional)	¼ cup soy sauce
Salt and pepper	1 cube beef bouillon
Vegetable oil	1 cup boiling water
1 (3-lb.) chicken, cleaned and sectioned	

---

1. Preheat the oven to 350°F.

2. In a small bowl, combine flour, ginger, salt, and pepper.

3. Heat oil in a skillet over high heat.

4. Coat chicken with seasoned flour, add to skillet, and brown on all sides. Arrange in a casserole dish.

5. Peel onions and slice thinly. Separate into rings and arrange over chicken. Sprinkle with soy sauce.

6. Dissolve bouillon cube in hot water. Pour in pan around chicken. Cover and bake for 45 minutes to 1 hour or until chicken is tender.

Southwestern Skillet Supper

Adapted from the recipe by the Idaho–Eastern Oregon Onion Committee

Yield: 6 servings

1 TB. vegetable oil	1 (16-oz.) can baked beans
1 lb. ground beef or turkey	1 (11-oz.) can corn, drained
1 medium onion, diced	Idaho instant mashed potatoes
2 tsp. chili powder	(enough for 4 servings)
¾ tsp. salt	½ cup shredded cheddar cheese
1 (16-oz.) can diced tomatoes	¼ cup chopped fresh cilantro

1. Heat oil in 12-inch skillet over medium-high heat. Add ground beef and onion, and cook until browned, stirring occasionally. Stir in chili powder and salt, and cook 1 minute longer. Stir in tomatoes with their liquid, baked beans, and corn. Cook over high heat until bubbling. Reduce heat to low, cover, and simmer for 10 minutes.

2. Meanwhile, prepare potatoes according to package directions for 4 servings. Stir in cheddar cheese and cilantro.

3. Top each meat mixture with ¼ cup potatoes, and serve.

German Onion Pie

Adapted from the recipe by the Idaho–Eastern Oregon Onion Committee

Yield: 8 servings

1½ cups plus 3 TB. flour, sifted	3 TB. butter or margarine
1½ tsp. salt	½ cup milk
1½ tsp. caraway seed	1½ cups sour cream
½ cup shortening	2 eggs, well beaten
2 or 3 TB. water	Crisp bacon curls
3 cups yellow onions, thinly sliced	

1. Preheat the oven to 425°F.

2. In a mixing bowl, combine 1½ cups flour, ¾ teaspoon salt, and caraway seed. Cut shortening into flour until mixture resembles small peas or coarse cornmeal. Stir in water lightly with a fork until mixture adheres and follows the fork around the bowl.

3. Turn dough onto a floured board and roll to ⅛-inch thickness. Fit into a 10-inch pie pan, and bake for 10 minutes or until lightly browned. Remove pastry shell from the oven and reduce the temperature to 325°F.

4. In a skillet, sauté onions in butter until lightly browned. Spoon into baked pastry shell. Add milk, 1¼ cups sour cream, and remaining ¾ teaspoon salt to beaten eggs.

5. In a small bowl, blend remaining 3 tablespoons flour with remaining ¼ cup sour cream. Combine with egg mixture and pour over onions.

6. Bake for 30 minutes or until firm in the center. Garnish with crisp bacon curls.

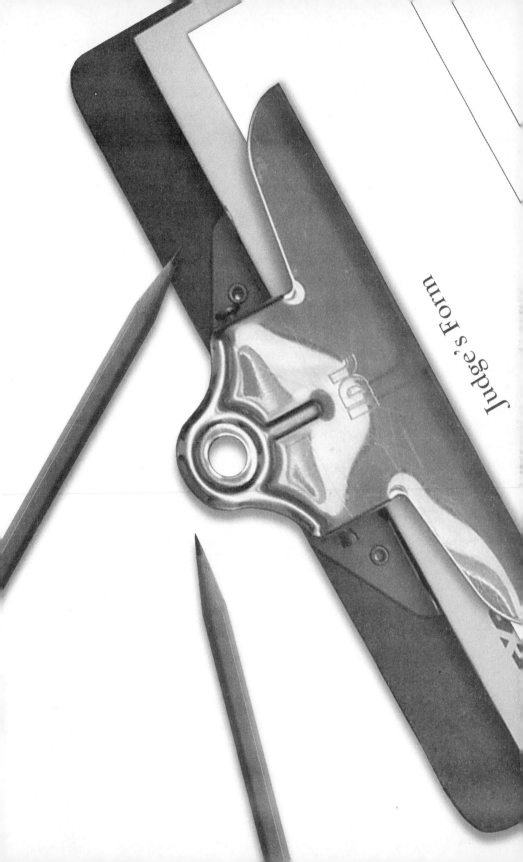

POTATO DAYS FESTIVAL

Barnesville, Minnesota
August
1-800-525-4901
www.potatodays.com

Down-home country fun awaits in Barnesville, Minnesota, as the local spud is the star attraction at the annual Potato Days Festival. Rated as one of the best festivals in the country by *U.S. News & World Report,* the Barnesville Potato Days Festival is the quintessential festival in small-town USA. Also recognized nationwide as one of the best potato-producing areas in the country, Barnesville is proud of its potato heritage, which it is pleased to share with the rest of the country through 2 days of *spud*tacular excitement.

A perfect weekend getaway for the entire family, young and old will enjoy endless activities from morning until night. The festival, originating in the late 1930s, is a combination of traditional foods with today's lifestyle. And there's something for everyone, from the thrilling Potato Picking and Peeling Contests, to the Miss Tator Tot Pageant, to the Mashed Potato Wrestling, to the specialized art of Mashed Potato Sculpturing.

Along with the festive assortment of additional potato-theme contests—Mr. and Mrs. Potato Head, Dress a Potato, Mashed Potato Eating, and Strongman Contest—the Potato Days Festival offers an appetizing menu of potato favorites. Begin the morning with the KC's Potato Pancake Feed. The Norwegian influence is unmistakable in the "Spud"riffic Smorgasbord at the Fabulous Food Court, which includes lefse (a soft Norwegian flatbread similar to a tortilla made with potato, milk, and flour, and cooked on a griddle), potato dumplings, potato sausage, baked potatoes, potato pancakes, and potato soup. In addition, participants are invited to display their culinary talents and perfect potato recipes as part of the National Lefse Cook-Off and Potato Salad Cook-Off competitions.

According to festival attendees, what particularly stands out at the festival is its devotion to the potato. Virtually everything you could possibly do to a potato is done at the festival's 2 days: picking, peeling, tossing, frying, racing, baking—but most of all, enjoying!

(Potato Days Festival)

Award-Winning Lefse

Adapted from the recipe by Lorraine Brusven

---

3 cups hot, mashed, cooked, peeled potatoes

⅓ cup butter, at room temperature

⅓ cup whipping cream

2 tsp. sugar

1 tsp. salt

1¾ cups all-purpose flour

---

1. In a large bowl, beat potatoes, butter, cream, sugar, and salt with an electric mixer for 2 or 3 minutes. Cover and chill in the refrigerator 4 to 24 hours.

2. On a lightly floured surface, sprinkle chilled potatoes with ¾ cup flour. Knead 8 to 10 minutes. Gradually knead remaining 1 cup flour into potatoes.

3. Divide into 24 portions, and shape each into 1½- to 2-inch balls. Chill in refrigerator.

4. On lightly floured surface, flatten each ball into a 3-inch circle. (Add flour if needed.)

5. Roll lefse around rolling pin, and transfer to a hot, ungreased griddle or nonstick skillet. Cook 1 or 2 minutes over medium-high heat or until brown spots appear. Turn and cook 1 additional minute.

Mom's Award-Winning Potato Salad

Adapted from the recipe by Anna Kiebke

Dressing:

1½ cups Miracle Whip Lite

¾ cup half-and-half or whole milk

2½ tsp. mustard

2 tsp. salt

¾ tsp. pepper

Salad:

6 cups potatoes (6 or 7 medium; red potatoes work best), cooked, peeled, and diced

1 large onion, chopped

2 cups celery, chopped

8 to 10 radishes, chopped

5 to 7 eggs, boiled and diced

1 cucumber, peeled and diced (optional)

Hard-boiled egg slices

Paprika

1. In a mixing bowl, combine Miracle Whip, half-and-half, mustard, salt, and pepper until smooth. Set dressing aside.

2. In a large bowl, combine potatoes, onion, celery, radishes, eggs, and cucumber (if using). Mix with dressing until well coated.

3. Top with slices of hard-boiled egg and sprinkle with paprika.

Note: This salad is best if made the night before or 5 or 6 hours before serving.

Award-Winning Potato Salad

Adapted from the recipe by Carolyn Boone

---

2 lb. potatoes, peeled and diced	1 onion, chopped
6 eggs, boiled, peeled, and diced	1 TB. mustard
1½ cups Miracle Whip	1½ TB. sugar
⅓ cup half-and-half	Salt and pepper

---

1. Dice potatoes into a saucepan, add water, and cook on medium heat until fork soft. Add eggs and continue to cook until incorporated. Remove from heat and let cool.

2. In a mixing bowl, combine Miracle Whip, half-and-half, onion, mustard, sugar, salt, and pepper. Add potatoes and eggs. Mix well.

3. Cover the bowl and let chill in refrigerator before serving.

Award-Winning Potato Clam Soup

Adapted from the recipe by Amy Kiebke Emerson

---

2 (10-oz.) cans potato soup	Salt and pepper
1 (14-oz.) can evaporated milk	1 or 2 TB. butter
1 small onion	1 or 2 small potatoes, peeled, cooked, and diced
1 small bunch scallions, chopped	
Crumbled bacon	2 (6-oz.) cans minced clams

---

1. In a large saucepan over medium heat, mix together potato soup, evaporated milk, onion, scallions, bacon, salt, pepper, butter, potatoes. Bring to low boil.

2. Add clams.

Potato Dumplings

Adapted from the recipe by Our Savior's Lutheran Church Ladies

---

5 lb. potatoes, peeled   Salt

Flour   Ham juice

---

1. Finely shred raw potatoes in a food processor.

2. Add flour to potatoes by the handful until mixture has consistency of dough. Mix in a little salt.

3. Shape potato dough into small balls with your hands.

4. In a saucepan, bring ham juice to a boil. Drop dumplings into ham juice, and boil about 20 minutes. Serve hot with melted butter.

GILROY GARLIC FESTIVAL

Gilroy, California
July
408-842-1625
www.gilroygarlicfestival.com

The Gilroy Garlic Festival began when Dr. Rudy Melone, then president of Gavilan College, read an article in mid-1978 about a garlic festival in Arleux, France. This community of just several thousand people claimed to be the Garlic Capital of the World because their 3-day event drew nearly 80,000 people to sample their garlic soup. Dr. Melone believed Gilroy, California, was the "Garlic Capital of the World" and decided to prove it. In 1979, Dr. Melone spearheaded a group that incorporated the Gilroy Garlic Festival Association, and the garlic festival was born.

From Cajun to Thai cooking, from garlic ice cream to escargot, you can find it all at the famous Gilroy Garlic Festival. Vendors throughout California vie for booths at the prestigious festival. Carefully selected and screened, festival committee members offer visitors the best variety anywhere.

The highlight of the event is the prestigious Great Garlic Cook-Off. It also happens to be one of the most well-known cooking contests in the country. Every December, the Gilroy Garlic Festival announces to America that it's looking for the best garlic recipes. Hundreds of amateur chefs respond with their recipe favorites ranging from soups to desserts and from every kind of cuisine. Recent winners have included Basil and Garlic–Stuffed Sea Scallops wrapped in Prosciutto and served with a Spicy Citrus Beurre Blanc and Garlic Seafood Soup.

The most delicious-sounding recipes, approximately 50, are sent to a professional food consultant, who makes the final selection of the 8 cook-off recipes. These finalists' recipes are those considered to make the most interesting and exciting contest. The consultant prepares each recipe to ensure correct measurements and use of ingredients.

The finalists come to Gilroy in July to prepare their recipes in front of the public. By noon, celebrity judges pick their favorites. The winner of the Great Garlic Cook-Off is appropriately honored with a crown of garlic and goes home $1,000 richer.

For garlic tips and new recipes, the Great Garlic Cook-Off Stage is the place you want to be.

(Gilroy Garlic Festival)

Garlic Seafood Soup

Adapted from the recipe by Ginger Moreno

Yield: 6 to 8 servings

1½ lb. mussels	1 medium tomato, finely diced
1½ lb. clams	½ cup clam broth
1½ lb. red snapper fillets	4 limes (1 juiced for broth, 2 or 3 cut into wedges for serving)
½ cup extra-virgin olive oil	
½ cup grated fresh ginger	3 TB. cilantro leaves, finely minced
1 cup finely minced garlic (about 2 heads)	1½ tsp. saffron
	2 cups lite coconut milk
1 cup finely minced sweet onion	1 jalapeño pepper
1 red bell pepper, finely diced	1 ripe or overripe banana, thinly sliced
1 yellow bell pepper, finely diced	Salt and pepper

1. De-beard mussels if needed. Scrub clams. Cut snapper into 2-inch pieces. Set seafood aside.

2. In a 12-inch nonstick skillet, heat ¼ cup olive oil over medium-high heat. Add ginger, ½ garlic, and onion. Add red and yellow bell pepper and tomato, and cook for 5 minutes. Turn heat to warm and cover.

3. In a 3-quart saucepan, heat remaining olive oil over medium-high heat. When oil is hot, add remaining garlic, juice from 1 lime, clams, mussels, and clam broth. Cover and cook for 7 minutes. Uncover shellfish and discard any unopened clams and mussels.

4. Add saffron, coconut milk, snapper pieces, ½ cilantro, jalapeño, banana, and bell pepper mixture. Stir to combine, cover, and cook for 6 to 8 minutes.

5. Sprinkle soup with remaining cilantro. Remove jalapeño pepper, ladle soup into bowls, and serve with crusty bread and extra lime wedges.

Prosciutto, Feta, and Rosemary Stuffed Bellas

Adapted from the recipe by Jennifer A. Malfas

Yield: 6 first course or side dish, 2 per person

5 whole heads garlic	1½ cups feta cheese, crumbled
¼ cup olive oil, plus 4 to 6 TB. for drizzling	1 cup garlic toast crumbs (from the grocery deli section)
Salt and pepper	12 baby portobella mushroom caps
2 sprigs fresh rosemary	12 slices prosciutto
1½ TB. chopped fresh rosemary	3 or 4 TB. chicken stock
1 lemon (zest and juice)	

1. Slice tops off garlic heads, and place heads on a sheet of aluminum foil. Drizzle with 2 or 3 tablespoons olive oil, and season with salt and pepper. Place 2 sprigs rosemary over garlic, wrap tightly in aluminum foil, and roast in the oven for 1 hour.

2. Remove roasted garlic from the oven, and squeeze pulp from heads into a bowl. Add ¼ cup olive oil, chopped rosemary, lemon zest, juice from ½ lemon, feta cheese, and garlic toast crumbs. Season with salt and pepper.

3. Remove stems from cleaned mushroom caps and fill with stuffing mixture. Wrap with 1 prosciutto slice, and place in a greased baking dish. Drizzle with 2 or 3 tablespoons olive oil, and season with salt and pepper.

4. When all mushrooms are in baking dish, pour in just enough chicken stock to cover the bottom. Cover with aluminum foil, and bake at 400°F for 15 minutes.

5. Remove from oven, spoon pan juices over mushrooms, re-cover, and bake for 10 to 15 more minutes. Baste with pan juices one more time and then broil, uncovered, for 2 or 3 minutes until prosciutto is brown and crisp.

Seafood Cakes with Citrus Salsa and Chipotle Aioli

Adapted from the recipe by Beth Royals

Yield: 6 servings

Seafood Cakes:

4 TB. unsalted butter

2 ribs celery, finely chopped

1 TB. minced garlic

½ lb. sea scallops, chopped

½ lb. cod fillets, chopped

1 (6-oz.) can lump crabmeat, drained

⅓ cup breadcrumbs

½ cup mayonnaise

2 TB. chopped cilantro

½ tsp. Old Bay seasoning

¼ tsp. salt

¼ tsp. black pepper

Citrus Salsa:

1 (15.25-oz.) can pineapple tidbits, drained and chopped

1 (11-oz.) can Mandarin orange segments, drained and chopped

1 TB. lime juice

1 TB. fresh cilantro, chopped

1 tsp. minced garlic

Chipotle Aioli:

1 cup mayonnaise

2 tsp. finely chopped chipotle peppers in adobo sauce

1 tsp. Worcestershire sauce

2 TB. bottled chili sauce

2 tsp. minced garlic

Fresh cilantro sprigs

1. Heat 2 tablespoons butter in a large sauté pan over medium heat. Cook celery and garlic, stirring until softened, about 2 minutes. Add chopped scallops and cod, stirring until cooked through and no longer opaque. Remove from heat, drain well, and stir in crabmeat.

2. In a large bowl, combine breadcrumbs, mayonnaise, cilantro, Old Bay seasoning, salt, and pepper. Add seafood, and fold in with a spatula.

3. In a bowl, combine pineapple, Mandarin oranges, lime juice, cilantro, and minced garlic.

4. In another bowl, combine mayonnaise, chipotle peppers, Worcester-shire sauce, chili sauce, and minced garlic.

5. Heat 1 tablespoon butter in a large sauté pan over medium heat. Form seafood mixture into 6 equally sized cakes or patties. Cook 3 cakes for about 3 minutes per side, until golden brown. Remove to a paper towel–lined plate. Add remaining 1 tablespoon butter and cook remaining cakes.

6. Spoon aioli into a plastic baggie, cut a small hole in one corner, and drizzle a zigzag of aioli on each plate. Top with a seafood cake. Place salsa and cilantro sprig on the side to garnish.

Basil and Garlic–Stuffed Sea Scallops with Prosciutto

Adapted from the recipe by Mary Beth Harris-Murphree

Yield: 6 servings

24 to 30 garlic cloves, skin on	1 tsp. salt
½ cup olive oil	½ tsp. black pepper
Pinch sea salt	3 TB. butter
Pinch coarse black pepper	⅔ cup chardonnay (or your favorite white wine)
2 lb. sea scallops (24 to 30)	
Small fresh basil leaves (1 per scallop; reserve extra for garnish)	2 TB. fresh lime juice
	2 TB. fresh lemon juice
Thinly sliced prosciutto (enough to wrap the outside of each scallop)	1 TB. orange zest, freshly grated
	½ tsp. cayenne
⅓ cup flour	¾ cup heavy cream
¼ tsp. paprika	¼ cup unsalted butter, cut into pieces

1. Preheat the oven to 250°F.

2. Place garlic cloves in a small, ovenproof dish, and drizzle with ½ cup olive oil, a pinch sea salt, and a pinch coarse black pepper. Cover and bake for 40 minutes, turning cloves over every now and then. Remove from oven and let garlic cool before carefully removing thin outer skins from each clove.

3. While garlic roasts, lay scallops on a flat, clean work surface. Place your hand on top of each scallop, and using a thin sharp knife, cut a small pocket into the side of each scallop, taking care not to cut all the way through.

4. Wrap 1 roasted garlic clove with 1 basil leaf and then insert gently into pocket of each scallop. Wrap sides of each stuffed scallop with 1 thin slice prosciutto to ensure garlic stays inside scallop; use a large toothpick to secure. Set aside.

5. In a medium shallow dish, combine flour, paprika, salt, and black pepper. Carefully toss stuffed scallops in flour, coating all sides.

6. In a large sauté pan over medium heat, melt 3 tablespoons butter. Add scallops gently and sauté for 3 or 4 minutes per side. Remove from the pan and keep warm until ready to serve.

7. In a medium saucepan, combine wine, lime juice, lemon juice, orange zest, and cayenne. Heat over medium-high heat and let simmer until reduced by ½. Stir in cream, and reduce heat to medium. Simmer for 8 to 10 minutes to reduce by ½ again. Turn heat to high and whisk in cold butter pieces until all butter is well incorporated. Keep warm.

8. To serve, place stuffed and wrapped sea scallops on a large platter and drizzle with Spicy Citrus Beurre Blanc Sauce. Garnish with any remaining basil leaves, if desired.

Grilled Candied-Garlic Salmon on Crispy Rice Noodles

Adapted from the recipe by Joann Donangelo

Yield: 6 servings

2 TB. Asian fish sauce

3 TB. lime juice

2 cloves garlic, pressed or minced

2 tsp. ginger, minced

2 tsp. curry paste

6 (6-oz.) salmon fillets

10 cloves garlic, sliced very thin

½ cup water

½ cup white wine

½ cup sugar

2 TB. butter

Vegetable oil

8 oz. dried rice noodles (maifun or rice sticks)

½ cup shallots, thinly sliced

Flour

1 clove garlic, pressed

2½ TB. candied garlic syrup

⅓ cup soy sauce

2 TB. lime juice

¼ cup water

½ cup snap peas, julienned

2 sliced green onions

8 cups baby Asian greens

Salt and pepper

1. Place fish sauce, lime juice, 2 cloves pressed or minced garlic, ginger, and curry paste in a resealable plastic bag and mix together. Add salmon and refrigerate for about 1 hour.

2. Prepare candied garlic by combining 10 cloves sliced garlic, water, white wine, sugar, and butter in a small saucepan. Simmer for 10 minutes or until syrupy; garlic should not be mushy. Remove garlic to cool. Reserve syrup for dressing.

3. Heat oil in deep-fry pan or wok, and fry rice noodles according to the package directions, a few at a time, draining on paper towels. (They'll look like Styrofoam.) Set aside. Keep oil hot.

4. Coat shallots with flour, and fry until golden and crisp. Drain on paper towels and set aside.

5. Combine 1 clove pressed garlic, candied garlic syrup, soy sauce, and lime juice to make dressing. Add water to taste, if needed. Set aside.

6. Mix snap peas, green onions, and greens in a bowl.

7. Heat the grill to medium-high.

8. Remove salmon from marinade and grill about 5 minutes per side.

9. Toss greens with dressing and divide among 6 plates. Top each serving with crispy noodles, followed by a serving of salmon. Top each salmon with fried shallots, candied garlic, and sliced scallions. Season with salt and pepper.

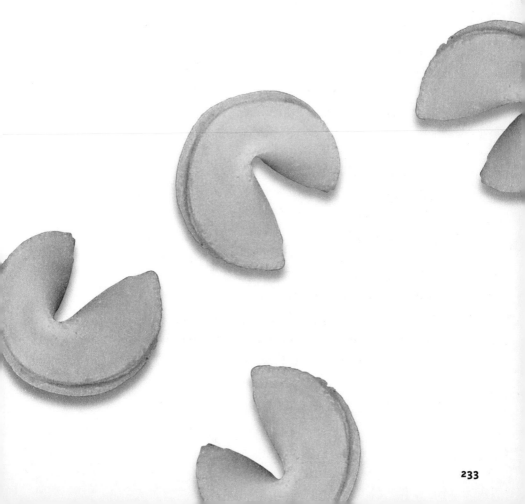

PONCA CITY HERB FESTIVAL

Ponca City, Oklahoma
June
580-762-7284 (Dianne Clark) or 580-718-0027 (Betty Caveny)
www.poncacityherbfestival.net

Imagine yourself strolling along winding paths in lush, herb-laden gardens with beautiful, soothing music wafting through the air. This is the scene at the annual Ponca City Herb Festival held every June in Ponca City, Oklahoma. Hosted by the Sage, Rosemary and Thyme Garden Club, the festival was founded by club member Mary Anne Potter in 1993 to promote public education of herbal gardening. Nestled in the 10-acre historical Cann Memorial Botanical Gardens, the Ponca City Herb Festival provides local citizens and visitors alike with a sanctuary of plants, flowers, and herbs to absorb and relish. By staging the festival at the Cann Memorial Garden, the Garden Club hopes to heighten public awareness of all Ponca City public gardens and to raise funds for their continuation.

Yearly attendance at the Ponca City Herb Festival is estimated at well over 20,000 visitors. Some of the treasures guests can marvel over and purchase include extraordinary herb plants, primitive birdhouses, yard ornaments, potting sheds, quilts, herbal vinegars and oils, handmade baskets, candles, soaps, furniture, potpourris, and stoneware from the more than 95 festival vendors from Oklahoma, Texas, Kansas, Colorado, and Arkansas.

Need an herb education? That's available, too, as the Ponca City Herb Festival offers a long list of seminars covering various topics from making herbal bath products and growing your own herbs, to herb and wildflower landscaping and herbal cooking. Festival founder Mary Anne teaches classes on how herbs and spices play a vital role in Italian cooking. Everett Taylor, a noted beekeeper from Oklahoma, presents a seminar on how bees are beneficial to one's garden and health. And Sandra Goodson shares her vast knowledge on chilies and spices and offers practical advice on the art of growing peppers.

(Ponca City Herb Festival)

Cinnamon Tea

Adapted from the recipe by Dianne Clark and the Ponca City Herb Festival

1 (12-oz.) pkg. Red Hots	1 tsp. cloves
20 cups water	12 oz. frozen cranberry juice, thawed
3 cups sugar	12 oz. frozen pineapple-orange juice, thawed
1 tsp. cinnamon	6 oz. frozen limeade, thawed

1. Soak Red Hots in about 4 cups water.

2. In a bowl, combine sugar, cinnamon, and cloves. Add cranberry juice, pineapple-orange juice, limeade, and Red Hot mixture.

3. When ready to heat, add remaining 16 cups water and heat in a percolator.

Herb Cheese Bread

Adapted from the recipe by Dianne Clark and the Ponca City Herb Festival

Yield: 1 loaf

1 cup mayonnaise	1 tsp. garlic salt
1 cup sour cream	½ (1-oz.) pkg. ranch dressing mix
1 TB. dried parsley	2 cups shredded mozzarella cheese
1 tsp. dried oregano	1 loaf French bread, sliced

1. Preheat the oven to 350°F.

2. In a bowl, combine mayonnaise, sour cream, parsley, oregano, garlic salt, ranch dressing mix, and cheese. Spread on French bread slices.

3. Bake bread for 15 minutes or until cheese is melted.

Mary Anne's Italian Chicken Salad

Adapted from the recipe by Mary Anne Potter and the Ponca City Herb Festival

---

10 cups coarsely shredded cooked chicken (from about 3 purchased roasted whole chickens)

2 cups roasted red and yellow bell peppers, drained, patted dry, and coarsely chopped

1¼ cups paper-thin slices red onion

¾ cup chopped fresh Italian parsley leaves

¾ cup slivered almonds, toasted

½ cup drained capers

Salt and freshly ground black pepper

24 butter lettuce leaves (from about 3 large heads)

1½ cups Red Wine Vinaigrette (recipe follows)

1 (4-oz.) piece Parmesan cheese, shaved with vegetable peeler

---

1. Toss chicken, bell peppers, onion, parsley, almonds, and capers in a large bowl with enough vinaigrette to moisten. Season chicken salad with salt and pepper. (Chicken salad can be prepared 4 hours ahead and refrigerated. Just before serving, spoon salad into lettuce cups.)

2. Arrange 1 large lettuce cup and 1 small lettuce cup on each plate, overlapping slightly. Spoon chicken salad into lettuce cups. Drizzle with Red Wine Vinaigrette, sprinkle with Parmesan cheese, and serve.

Red Wine Vinaigrette

Yield: 1¾ cups

½ cup red wine vinegar

¼ cup lemon juice

2 tsp. honey

2 tsp. salt

Freshly ground black pepper

1 cup olive oil

---

1. Combine vinegar, lemon juice, honey, salt, and pepper in a blender or food processor.

2. With the blender still running, gradually add oil and blend until emulsified.

Green Rice

Adapted from the recipe by Dianne Clark and the Ponca City Herb Festival

¾ cup green onions, sliced thin	¼ cup fresh parsley, minced
3 TB. oil	2 cups canned chicken broth
1 cup rice, uncooked	1 tsp. salt
½ cup green peppers, minced	¼ tsp. pepper

1. Preheat the oven to 350°F.

2. In a saucepan, cook onions in oil until soft but not brown. Add rice, green peppers, parsley, chicken broth, salt, and pepper.

3. Pour rice into a 2-quart baking pan with a cover. Bake for 30 minutes. Toss lightly with a fork before serving.

Shrimp and Noodles in Parmesan Dill Sauce

Adapted from the recipe by Dianne Clark and the Ponca City Herb Festival

Yield: 5 or 6 servings

4 oz. wide egg noodles

1 (7-oz.) pkg. fresh or frozen shelled shrimp, thawed if frozen

¼ cup chopped onion

3 TB. butter

3 TB. all-purpose flour

½ tsp. salt

½ tsp. dried dill weed

2 cups whole milk

⅓ cup grated Parmesan cheese

½ (3-oz.) can french-fried onion rings

Dill sprigs (optional)

1. Preheat the oven to 350°F.

2. Cook noodles according to package directions. Drain and set aside.

3. Cook shrimp until firm and red in color, or according to package directions. Drain and set aside.

4. In a saucepan, cook onion in butter until tender but not brown. Stir in flour, salt, and dill weed. Add milk all at once, and cook, stirring, until thickened and bubbly. Stir in Parmesan cheese. Gently stir in noodles and shrimp.

5. Turn mixture into a 1½-quart casserole dish. Bake, covered, until heated through, about 30 minutes. Sprinkle french-fried onion rings around the edges of casserole. Bake, uncovered, for 5 more minutes. Garnish with sprigs of dill (if using).

LOS ANGELES TOFU FESTIVAL

Los Angeles, California
August
213-473-3030
www.tofufest.org

Tofu, or bean curd, is made by coagulating soy milk and then pressing the resulting curds into blocks, similar to how cheese is made from milk.

Evidence of tofu goes as far back as 220 C.E. According to archaeologists, tofu was made in northern China during the Eastern/Later Han period (22 to 220 C.E.). In Japan, the first mention of tofu came in 1183. It wasn't until 1489 that the characters used for the current word *tofu* were first written in Japan.

In America, the earliest known reference to tofu was in 1770, when Benjamin Franklin wrote a letter describing the unique food. Later, in the 1800s, the first tofu manufacturer in America, Wo Sing & Co., was founded to serve the throng of Chinese immigrants arriving in the United States. Soon other tofu companies emerged, including the notable Quong Hop & Co., the oldest existing tofu maker in America today.

Even with decades of tofu production in the United States, it wasn't until 1958 that tofu was first sold in a U.S. supermarket. Nearly 40 years later, the Little Tokyo Service Center (LTSC) decided to create a new fund-raising dinner for supporters to attend. In 1995, LTSC Board members brainstormed and came up with a brilliant food festival, which would later morph into the first Tofu Festival.

On August 10, 1996, with 30 food, health, and craft booths, 8,000 people turned out in Los Angeles for the first Tofu Festival, where patrons consumed more than 25,000 tofu dishes. Today, more than 25,000 visitors come to savor extraordinary tofu and soy dishes, as well other festival activities such as the Hi Tech Celebrity Chef Cooking Stage with robotic cameras and plasma screens; A Taste of Japan, the ever-popular Tofu Eating Contest; and plenty of live musical entertainment. Recently, the Food Network's *BBQ with Bobby Flay* captured the festival on television, as did the Travel Channel's *Taste of America*.

(Los Angeles Tofu Festival)

Tofu Spinach Mushroom Quiche

Adapted from the recipe by the Los Angeles Tofu Festival

Yield: 6 servings

1 (9-in.) unbaked pastry shell

3 large eggs, scrambled

1 (14-oz.) pkg. regular Hinoichi tofu, drained and chopped

1 cup shredded Swiss cheese

3 large mushrooms, sliced

½ bunch spinach, parboiled and chopped

Salt and pepper

1. Preheat the oven to 450°F. Bake pastry shell for 5 minutes and remove from the oven. Reduce heat to 325°F.

2. In a food processor, add eggs and process until smooth.

3. In a separate bowl, add tofu and fold in cheese, mushrooms, and spinach. Add eggs and with salt and pepper to taste.

4. Pour into baked pie shell and bake for 30 minutes or until a knife inserted in the center comes out clean.

Bagel Pizza with Tofu Topping

Adapted from the recipe by the Los Angeles Tofu Festival

Yield: 12 bagel pizzas

6 plain bagels, sliced in half

2 cups high-quality spaghetti sauce

1 (14-oz.) pkg. Hinoichi tofu, drained and finely crumbled

1½ cups mozzarella cheese, shredded

½ medium onion, thinly sliced

1 (4-oz.) can sliced black olives

1. Preheat the broiler.

2. Toast bagel slices for 1 minute.

3. In a medium bowl, mix spaghetti sauce with tofu. Spoon on top of toasted bagels. Top with cheese, onion, and olives.

4. Broil bagels for 5 minutes or until cheese is melted.

Soy Milk Somen

Adapted from the recipe by the Los Angeles Tofu Festival

Yield: 3 or 4 servings

1 egg, cooked and cut into julienne strips	Salt
1 (8-oz.) pkg. somen noodles	½ cucumber, peeled and sliced into julienne strips
2 cups soy milk	1 small tomato, sliced into 8 pieces
½ cup milk	

1. Beat 1 egg and fry in a skillet over medium heat forming a crepelike surface. Do not scramble. Remove from heat and let cool. When cool, slice egg into julienne strips.

2. Cook somen noodles according to package directions, rinse with cold water, and drain completely. Place into a serving bowl.

3. In a medium bowl, mix soy milk and milk. Season with salt, and pour into small bowls.

4. Garnish somen noodles with cucumber, egg, and tomato slices. Serve noodles with soy milk for dipping.

Kung Pao Tofu

Adapted from the recipe by the Los Angeles Tofu Festival

Yield: 4 to 6 servings

1 (14-oz.) pkg. Hinoichi Extra Firm tofu, drained	1 large bell pepper, cut into bite-size pieces
2 TB. cornstarch	1 green onion, chopped
1 TB. oyster sauce	3 TB. balsamic or Jin Jang vinegar
1 or 2 tsp. oil	1 TB. sake, or 1 TB. dry sherry
1 clove garlic, minced	1 TB. dark soy sauce
5 or 6 pieces dried red chili pepper, crushed	1 TB. sugar
	1 tsp. hot garlic chili sauce
1 stalk celery, chopped into bite-size pieces	2 TB. water
½ bamboo shoots, chopped into bite-size pieces	½ cup roasted whole cashew nuts (optional)

1. Drain tofu and place on a cutting board. Place another cutting board on top, and push down gently to squeeze out water but not crumble tofu. Cut tofu into blocks.

2. In a medium bowl, combine 1 tablespoon cornstarch and oyster sauce. Add tofu blocks to marinate.

3. Heat a wok or frying pan and add oil. Toss in garlic and red chili pepper. Add celery, takenoko, bell pepper, and green onion, and sauté.

4. Add tofu, and gently pan fry.

5. In a small bowl, mix vinegar, sake, soy sauce, sugar, and chili sauce. Add sauce to tofu mixture, and allow to simmer for a while.

6. In another small bowl mix remaining 1 tablespoon cornstarch and water and add to tofu mixture to thicken sauce.

7. Garnish with cashew nuts (if using), and serve hot with rice.

Seafood Tofu Gyoza

Adapted from the recipe by the Los Angeles Tofu Festival

Yield: 50 gyozas

¼ lb. shrimp, peeled, deveined, and rinsed	3 green onions, chopped
	1 tsp. salt
1 (14-oz.) pkg. regular Hinoichi tofu, drained and mashed	1 tsp. black pepper
5 large mushrooms, sliced	1 TB. plus ¼ cup soy sauce
¼ lb. Chinese cabbage, parboiled and chopped	1 tsp. sesame oil
	2 pkg. gyoza wrappers
4 cloves garlic, minced	1 TB. vegetable oil
1 TB. fresh gingerroot, minced	¼ cup rice wine vinegar
1 small onion, chopped	1 tsp. chili oil
½ bunch leek, chopped	

1. In a large mixing bowl, combine shrimp, tofu, mushrooms, Chinese cabbage, garlic, gingerroot, onion, leek, green onions, salt, pepper, 1 tablespoon soy sauce, and sesame oil. Form into 50 teaspoon-size meatballs.

2. Place 1 meatball in center of 1 gyoza wrapper, and fold wrapper in ½ (making a triangle), keeping meatball in the center. Seal wrapper by putting some water on the edges and closing tightly.

3. Preheat a frying pan with 1 tablespoon vegetable oil. Place wrapped gyozas in the pan, flattening bottom of gyozas so tips of triangle are pointing up. Cover and heat until cooked through.

4. Flip gyozas once, add 1 tablespoon water to the pan, and cover. Remove pan from heat and let steam for 3 to 5 minutes.

5. In a small bowl, combine rice wine vinegar, remaining ¼ cup soy sauce, and chili oil. Serve gyozas hot with dipping sauce.

Part 4

Desserts

GREAT AMERICAN PIE FESTIVAL

Celebration, Florida
April
847-371-0170
www.piecouncil.org/great.htm

Organized by the American Pie Council, which is dedicated to preserving the American pie heritage and promoting our weakness for the delectable dessert, the Great American Pie Festival encourages an awareness, enjoyment, and consumption of pies.

Today, visitors to the Great American Pie Festival in Celebration, Florida, can experience exciting venues that include Children's Pie Making, Cooking Demonstrations, Pie-Eating Contests, a Never-Ending Pie Buffet featuring award-winning pies, and the well-recognized National Pie Championships where amateur, professional, and commercial pie bakers compete for the best pies in the country.

Of course, pies can be enjoyed all year around, not just in April, when the festival is held. January is a great time to serve pies. According to the American Pie Council, January 23 is National Pie Day.

Pies have been served up since the days of the early Egyptians and Romans, who were the first to create pies, and they weren't just for dessert. According to historical documents, instead of a golden flakey crust, the Romans assembled the first pies using grass reeds to hold the filling, which was the only part of the pie consumed. The Romans are also credited with publishing the first pie recipe—a goat cheese and honey pie. It wasn't until the 1500s that fruit pies and tarts started appearing. In fact, Queen Elizabeth I is credited with making the first cherry pie.

Like many other celebrated food products, delicious pies made their way to America with the first English settlers. The early pioneers, taking after the Romans, continued to eat the pie filling and nothing more. During the American Revolution, the term *crust* began to emerge, and not long after, Americans were eating the entire pie.

Thanks to our early ancestors, pies have evolved to what they are today—the traditional American dessert.

(Great American Pie Festival)

Classic Cherry Pie

Adapted from the recipe by Valerie Enters

Yield: 1 pie

2 cups flour

3 tsp. confectioners' sugar

¼ cup butter

½ tsp. salt

½ cup Crisco Butter Flavor shortening

1 egg

2 tsp. vinegar

¼ cup ice water

4 cups drained Morello cherries, 1⅓ cups juice reserved

1¼ cups sugar

3 TB. tapioca

Pinch salt

Red gel food coloring

1. In a mixing bowl, blend flour, confectioners' sugar, butter, and ½ teaspoon salt. Cut in Crisco until mixture resembles cornmeal.

2. In a separate bowl, beat egg, and blend in vinegar and water. Sprinkle over flour mixture, toss with a fork, and chill about 1 hour before rolling.

3. Roll out 2 pie shells and place one in a 9-inch pie tin. Reserve the second for top crust.

4. Preheat the oven to 425°F.

5. In a mixing bowl, combine cherry juice, sugar, tapioca, salt, and a tiny dab of food coloring. Add cherries and pour filling into pie shell. Cover with top crust.

6. Bake for 15 minutes. Reduce the oven temperature to 350°F, and bake for 45 minutes or until golden.

Cherry Berry Surprise Pie

Adapted from the recipe by Emily Spaugh

Yield: 1 pie

1 cup sugar	1½ cups cherry pie filling
2 TB. cornstarch	3 cups all-purpose flour
1¼ tsp. salt	1 cup chilled Crisco shortening
2 TB. quick-cooking tapioca	6 TB. cold water
½ cup cherry juice	1 TB. white vinegar
1 cup blackberries	1 egg yolk, beaten
1½ cups strawberries, sliced	1 TB. unsalted butter, cut into small pieces

1. In a large bowl, mix together sugar, cornstarch, and 1/4 teaspoon salt.

2. In a separate small bowl, dissolve tapioca in cherry juice.

3. Add blackberries and strawberries to sugar-cornstarch mixture, and toss to mix. Add cherry juice and tapioca, and toss again to mix.

4. Add cherry pie filling, gently mix thoroughly, and set aside.

5. In a mixing bowl, combine flour and remaining 1 teaspoon salt. Using a pastry blender, cut in shortening until pieces are pea size.

6. In another bowl, mix water, vinegar, and beaten egg yolk. Sprinkle water-egg mixture over dry ingredients until it forms a ball. Press dough between hands to form a ball and divide in ½. Chill for 30 minutes.

7. Preheat the oven to 375°F.

8. Roll out 1 ball for bottom crust and place in a 9-inch pie pan. Pour filling into bottom piecrust, and spread butter pieces evenly over filling.

9. Roll out remaining crust into a 10-inch circle and cut into strips to make lattice top. Cover pie top with lattice. Trim strips even with the inside of bottom crust. Brush ends of strips with water. Fold excess dough over strips, pinching to seal. Crimp edges as desired.

10. Bake for 15 minutes, reduce heat to 350°F, and bake until crust is golden and filling juices are thick and glossy. Allow to cool before serving.

Peanut Butter Proposal Pie

Adapted from the recipe by Raine Gottess

Yield: 1 pie

18 Nutter Butter cookies, crushed fine	1 (8-oz.) tub Creamy Cool Whip
3½ TB. butter, melted	8 Reese's Peanut Butter Cups, chopped
1 (12-oz.) pkg. cream cheese, softened	¼ cup brown sugar
1½ cups confectioners' sugar	1 cup creamy peanut butter
1 TB. milk	½ (12-oz.) tub Cool Whip
1 tsp. vanilla extract	Crushed peanuts

1. In a bowl, mix crushed Nutter Butter cookies and melted butter until moist. Press mixture into a 9- or 10-inch deep-dish pie pan, and freeze 10 minutes to firm.

2. In a mixing bowl and with a handheld mixer, beat cream cheese, confectioners' sugar, milk, vanilla extract, and 8 ounces Cool Whip until blended. Spread ½ of mixture over crust.

3. Distribute 4 chopped Reese's Peanut Butter Cups over cream cheese–Cool Whip layer in crust, and freeze about 5 minutes.

4. To remaining cream cheese–Cool Whip mixture, add brown sugar and peanut butter. Blend well and spread over filling in crust.

5. Decorate with remaining 6 ounces Cool Whip, and add a sprinkle of crushed peanuts and remaining 4 chopped Reese's Peanut Butter Cups. Refrigerate 8 hours before serving.

Just Splenda'd
Raspberry Ripple Pie

Adapted from the recipe by Marles Reissland

Yield: 8 servings

Crust:

1 cup pastry flour

2 cups all-purpose flour

1 tsp. salt

½ tsp. baking powder

1 cup plus 1 TB. Crisco Butter Flavor shortening, chilled

⅓ cup ice cold water

1 TB. vinegar

1 egg, beaten

Pineapple Filling:

4 egg yolks, slightly beaten

1 TB. water

⅓ cup firmly packed cornstarch

1⅓ cups white chocolate chips

¼ tsp. salt

2 cups milk

1 (20-oz.) can crushed pineapple, juiced pack, ⅓ cup juice reserved

2 TB. butter

1 tsp. vanilla extract

Cream Cheese Filling:

1 (8-oz.) pkg. cream cheese

½ cup Splenda No Calorie Granulated

½ tsp. vanilla extract

Raspberry Filling:

⅓ cup Splenda No Calorie Granulated

1 TB. cornstarch

1 cup frozen raspberries, thawed

2 TB. raspberry juice

¼ tsp. almond extract

¼ tsp. red food coloring

Crème Fraîche Topping:

1 cup cold whipping cream

2 TB. Splenda No Calorie Granulated

⅓ cup sour cream

Fresh raspberries and/or mint leaves

1. To prepare crust: in a large bowl, combine pastry flour, all-purpose flour, salt, and baking powder. Cut in shortening with a pastry blender until mixture resembles cornmeal.

2. In a small bowl, mix water and vinegar with egg. Add liquid mixture, 1 tablespoon at a time, to flour mixture, tossing with a fork to form soft dough.

3. Shape dough into 3 discs. Wrap in plastic wrap and chill in refrigerator for 1 hour. Use 1 disc for this recipe.

4. Preheat the oven to 425°F.

5. Roll out 1 dough disc to fit a 9-inch pie pan. Adjust crust into pan, flute edge, and prick bottom. Bake for 15 to 20 minutes or until golden brown. Cool completely before filling.

6. *Pineapple Filling:* combine egg yolks and water in a small bowl. Stir in cornstarch, and set aside.

7. Combine white chocolate, salt, milk, and pineapple in saucepan. Cook and stir over medium heat until mixture almost boils. Reduce heat to low.

8. Slowly stir egg yolk mixture into chocolate-pineapple mixture. Cook and stir until thickened. Add butter and vanilla extract. Remove the pan from heat, and cover surface with plastic wrap. Refrigerate 30 minutes or longer, stirring once or twice.

9. *Cream Cheese Filling:* beat together cream cheese and Splenda until smooth.

10. Add vanilla extract and ⅓ cup reserved pineapple juice, mix well, and set aside.

11. *Raspberry Filling:* in a small bowl, combine Splenda and cornstarch.

12. In a small saucepan, mix together raspberries and raspberry juice. Stir in Splenda-cornstarch mixture. Cook over medium heat 3 or 4 minutes or until thickened. Remove from heat and stir in almond extract and red food coloring. Cool.

13. *Crème Fraîche Topping:* in a medium-size mixing bowl, beat cream with a handheld mixer on high speed until frothy. Add Splenda and beat until thickened. Fold in sour cream. Cover and refrigerate.

14. To assemble pie, spread Cream Cheese Filling over bottom of cool baked pie shell. Spread Raspberry Filling over Cream Cheese Filling. Spread Pineapple Filling over Raspberry Filling. Before serving, spoon Crème Fraîche Topping onto top of pie. Garnish with fresh raspberries and/or mint leaves. Refrigerate.

BANANA SPLIT FESTIVAL

Wilmington, Ohio
June
937-382-1965
www.bananasplitfestival.com

Welcome to Wilmington, Ohio—home to the world's first banana split and the well-received Banana Split Festival. It's here where thousands of devoted fans flock every June to sample the traditional banana split. They also come to relive the story of Ernest Hazard, the man who folks around Wilmington say is credited for creating the first banana split.

Although there's much debate on who actually created the well-known dessert, the people of Wilmington and their popular festival stand by their claim that they are, indeed, the originators of the banana split. According to local townsfolk, in 1907, Wilmington resident Hazard was trying to concoct a way to attract the Wilmington College students, who always came into Hazard's Restaurant. He decided to create a new dish to help spark sales. He took a long dessert dish and filled it with a peeled banana and three scoops of ice cream and added a drop of chocolate syrup, a little strawberry jam, and a few pieces of pineapple. On top of all of this, he sprinkled some ground nuts and garnished his creation with a mound of whipped cream and two red cherries.

The new dish went over extremely well. But what to call it? The "banana split" was Hazard's name for it, although many others, including Hazard's cousin Clifton, believed no one would ever walk in and ask for something called a banana split. Little did Hazard know he had created one of the most popular ice cream dishes in history.

At the annual Banana Split Festival, visitors arrive hungry, and well they should, as there's plenty to eat, including corn dogs, nachos, funnel cakes, elephant ears, sugar waffles, cotton candy, hamburgers, cheeseburgers, hot dogs, chili dogs, chili, shaved ice, and soft pretzels. There's also fried alligator, jambalaya, blackened chicken, butterfly pork chop sandwiches, BBQ pork, pork loin pita, tater wedges, rib eye steak sandwiches, curly and ribbon fries, BBQ beef, lemon shake-ups, homemade soda pop, gourmet coffee, kettle corn, sausage sandwiches, grilled chicken breasts, pizza, snow cones, slushies, roasted nuts, shredded chicken sandwiches, and BBQ hog wings.

Of course, the highlighted festival attraction is the banana split itself. At a "build your own" banana split booth, you can decide how many scoops you would like, and what variety of toppings you'd like to customize your dessert. And if you're still feeling hungry, don't forget to enter a chance to compete with others at the festival's popular Banana Split Eating Contest.

(*Banana Split Festival*)

Original Banana Split

Adapted from the recipe by Ernest Hazard in 1907

Yield: 1 serving

1 banana	Pineapple bits
3 scoops vanilla ice cream	Ground nuts
1 shot chocolate syrup	Whipped cream
Strawberry jam	2 red cherries

1. In a long dessert dish, arrange a peeled banana and ice cream. Add chocolate syrup, a little strawberry jam, and a few bits of pineapple.

2. Sprinkle with some ground nuts, and garnish with a mountain of whipped cream and 2 red cherries on the peak.

Banana Split Cake

Adapted from the recipe by the Banana Split Festival

Yield: 1 cake, about 25 servings

⅓ cup butter or margarine, softened	1 tsp. baking powder
1 cup sugar	¼ tsp. salt
1 egg	⅓ cup chopped walnuts
1 medium ripe banana, mashed	2 cups miniature marshmallows
½ tsp. vanilla extract	1 cup semisweet chocolate chips
1¼ cups all-purpose flour	⅓ cup maraschino cherries, quartered

1. Preheat the oven to 350°F. Grease a 13×9×2-inch baking pan.

2. In a mixing bowl, cream butter and sugar. Beat in egg, banana, and vanilla extract.

3. In a separate bowl, combine flour, baking powder, and salt. Stir dry ingredients into butter mixture. Add walnuts.

4. Spread batter evenly into the prepared pan. Bake for 20 minutes. Sprinkle with marshmallows, chocolate chips, and cherries, and bake for 10 minutes longer or until lightly browned. Cool on a wire rack, cut into squares, and serve.

GREAT WISCONSIN CHEESE FESTIVAL

Little Chute, Wisconsin
June
937-382-6000
www.littlechutewi.org/calendar_events/cheesefest.html

Wisconsin is synonymous with *cheese*, and where you find great cheese, you find great cheesecakes. This is particularly true at the Great Wisconsin Cheese Festival in Little Chute. Along with the great cheesecakes whipped up at the festival's acclaimed cheesecake contest, cheese lovers can also participate in a cheese curd eating competition, free cheese tastings, cheese carving demonstrations, a Big Cheese Parade, a Big Cheese Breakfast, carnival rides, and plenty of children's games and entertainment.

Since 1988, the first weekend in June has been a celebration in Little Chute. The Great Wisconsin Cheese Festival is a fun-filled 3-day event that celebrates the state's dairy industry and the local cheese producers of Little Chute.

In its first year, the festival received national attention for its cheese tasting contest between Wisconsin and New York. It all began when a story appeared in a local newspaper that questioned why a national cheese museum was placed in Rome, New York. When Wisconsin senator Walter John Chilsen penned a poem stating that Wisconsin, the Dairy State that makes the best cheese, should have been the site of the museum, New York responded by holding an impromptu "cheese-off." New York, of course, declared their cheese the winner, but Wisconsin cheese lovers wouldn't let it end there.

The citizens of Little Chute offered to hold a second cheese-off, this time at the 1st Annual Great Wisconsin Cheese Festival. The mayor of Rome, New York, Carl J. Eilenberg, accepted the invitation to attend, and the Cheese Festival sent him a plane ticket. In the contest, Wisconsin cheese won in all categories and was dubbed "Best Cheese in the USA." Mayor Eilenberg filed a protest, claiming the tasting was unfair because the cheeses were easily recognized as "Wisconsin" and "New York." He requested a blind testing on live television and proceeded to blindfold a TV reporter on the scene. The reporter picked Wisconsin cheese as the best.

Today, the Great Wisconsin Cheese Festival continues to serve up some of the best cheeses on the planet. Come see and taste for yourself by visiting this famous festival in the little town of Little Chute.

(Great Wisconsin Cheese Festival)

White Chocolate Raspberry Cheesecake

Adapted from the recipe by Becky Dawson

Yield: 1 pie

2 cups crushed Oreo cookies	¼ tsp. salt
4 TB. butter	3 egg whites
2 (6-oz.) pkg. Nestlé premier white baking bars	1 whole egg
½ cup heavy cream	1 (10-oz.) pkg. frozen raspberries
2 (8-oz.) pkg. cream cheese	¼ cup sugar
1 TB. lemon juice	2 TB. cornstarch

1. Preheat the oven to 350°F.

2. Add butter to crushed Oreos, blending until combined. Press over bottom and ⅔ up the sides of a 10-inch springform pan.

3. In small saucepan over low heat, melt white chocolate with cream until smooth.

4. In a large bowl, mix cream cheese, lemon juice, and salt. Blend in white chocolate mixture. Beat in egg whites and whole egg.

5. Pour batter into crust, and bake for 35 minutes.

6. Add frozen raspberries, sugar, and cornstarch in a food processor and blend until smooth.

7. When pie is finished baking, run a knife around the edge of pan to loosen and then cool completely in pan on a rack. (Pie will continue to set as it cools.) Before serving at room temperature or chilled, drizzle with raspberry sauce.

White Chocolate Lime Cheesecake

Adapted from the recipe by Jean Landreman

Yield: 1 pie

¼ cup melted margarine	1 tsp. vanilla extract
1 cup flour	1 (10-oz.) bag white chocolate chips, melted
1½ cups sugar	
4 (8-oz.) pkg. cream cheese	¼ cup fresh lime juice
1 cup sugar	Melted white chocolate
4 eggs	Whipped cream
	Lime wedges

1. Preheat the oven to 350°F. Grease a 9-inch springform pan.

2. In a mixing bowl, blend together melted margarine, flour, and ½ cup sugar. Pat crust into the prepared pan.

3. In a mixing bowl, blend cream cheese and remaining 1 cup sugar. Add eggs and vanilla extract, and mix well.

4. Mix ½ of batter with melted white chocolate chips and pour in the pan. Mix remaining ½ of batter with lime juice and pour into the pan over other ½ of mixture. Bake for 1 hour.

5. Garnish drizzle melted white chocolate, whipped cream, and/or lime wedges.

Wisconsin Springtime Rhubarb Delight Cheesecake

Adapted from the recipe by Jayne M. Vosters

Yield: 1 pie

2½ cups thinly sliced fresh or frozen rhubarb	2 cups (16 oz.) sour cream
⅓ cup plus ½ cup sugar	1 TB. cornstarch
2 TB. orange juice	2 tsp. vanilla extract
1¼ cups graham cracker crumbs	½ tsp. salt
¼ cup butter, melted	3 eggs, lightly beaten
3 (8-oz.) pkg. cream cheese, softened	8 (1-oz.) squares white baking chocolate, melted

1. Preheat the oven to 350°F. Grease a 9-inch springform pan.

2. In a large saucepan over high heat, bring rhubarb, ⅓ cup sugar, and orange juice to a boil. Reduce heat, cook and stir until thickened and rhubarb is tender, and set aside.

3. In a bowl, combine graham cracker crumbs and butter. Press onto the bottom of the prepared pan. Place the pan on a baking sheet, and bake for 7 to 9 minutes or until lightly browned. Cool on a wire rack.

4. In a large mixing bowl, beat cream cheese, sour cream, cornstarch, vanilla extract, salt, and remaining ½ cup sugar until smooth. Add eggs and beat just until combined. Fold in white chocolate.

5. Pour ½ of filling into crust. Top with ½ of rhubarb sauce. Cut through batter with a knife to gently swirl rhubarb. Layer with remaining filling and rhubarb sauce, and cut through top layers with a knife to gently swirl rhubarb.

6. Place pan on a double thickness of heavy-duty aluminum foil about 16 inches square. Securely wrap foil around pan, place in a large baking pan, and add 1 inch hot water to the larger pan. Bake for 60 to 70 minutes or until center is almost set.

7. Cool on a wire rack for 10 minutes. Carefully run a knife around the edge of the pan to loosen, and cool 1 hour longer. Cover and chill overnight. Remove sides of pan. Refrigerate any leftovers.

Note: If using frozen rhubarb, measure rhubarb while still frozen and then thaw completely. Drain in a colander, but do not press out liquid.

Turtle Cheesecake

Adapted from the recipe by Becky Dawson

Yield: 1 pie

2 cups vanilla wafer crumbs	½ cup sugar
6 TB. Parkay margarine, melted	1 tsp. vanilla extract
1 (14-oz.) bag Kraft caramels	2 eggs
1 (5-oz.) can evaporated milk	½ cup semi-sweet chocolate pieces, melted
1 cup chopped pecans, toasted	
2 (8-oz.) pkg. Philadelphia Cream Cheese, softened	Whipped cream (optional)
	Cherries (optional)

1. Preheat the oven to 350°F.

2. In a medium bowl, combine vanilla wafer crumbs and melted margarine. Press mixture onto the bottom and sides of a 9-inch springform pan. Bake for 10 minutes.

3. In 1½-quart heavy saucepan over low heat, melt caramels with milk, stirring frequently until smooth. Pour over crust. Top with pecans.

4. In a large bowl and with an electric mixer on medium speed, combine cream cheese, sugar, and vanilla extract until well blended. Add eggs one at a time, mixing well after each addition. Blend in chocolate. Pour batter over pecans, and bake for 40 minutes.

5. Loosen cake from the rim of the pan, and cool before removing the rim. Chill cheesecake, and garnish with whipped cream, additional chopped nuts, and cherries before serving, if desired.

Wisconsin Delicious Caramel Apple Cheesecake

Adapted from the recipe by Tim De Groot

Yield: 1 pie

1 cup graham cracker crumbs	¾ tsp. vanilla extract
3 TB. plus 1 cup sugar	2½ cups chopped and peeled Wisconsin Delicious apples
1 tsp. ground cinnamon	
¼ cup melted butter	1 TB. lemon juice
2 TB. finely chopped pecans	6 TB. caramel ice cream topping
3 (8-oz.) pkg. cream cheese, softened	Whipped cream
3 eggs	2 TB. chopped pecans

1. Preheat the oven to 350°F. Lightly grease a 9-inch springform pan.

2. In a bowl, combine graham cracker crumbs, 3 tablespoons sugar, ½ teaspoon cinnamon, butter, and pecans. Press onto the bottom of the prepared pan, and bake for 10 minutes. Set aside to cool.

3. In a mixing bowl, beat cream cheese and ¾ cup sugar until smooth. Add eggs one at a time, and beat with an electric mixer on low just until combined. Stir in vanilla extract, and pour batter over cooled crust.

4. Toss chopped apples with lemon juice, remaining ¼ cup sugar, and remaining ½ teaspoon cinnamon. Spoon over filling and bake for 55 to 60 minutes or until center is almost set.

5. Cool cheesecake on a wire rack for 10 minutes and then carefully run a knife around the edge of the pan to loosen. Drizzle cheesecake with 4 tablespoons caramel ice cream topping. Cool for 1 hour and then chill overnight.

6. Remove the sides of the pan. Just before serving, garnish with whipped cream, drizzle with remaining caramel, and sprinkle with pecans.

AUSTIN CHOCOLATE FESTIVAL

Austin, Texas
March
1-800-834-3498
www.austinchocolatefestival.com

If you're a chocoholic, the Austin Chocolate Festival, a recently created festival in Austin, Texas, is the place to be in March when more than 25 chocolatiers, bakeries, pastisseries, restaurants, and caterers come together under one roof to share their love for the sweet stuff.

Highlights of the festival include publicly judged contests in 13 categories ranging from the best chocolate sculptures to the most creative dessert. There's also a Gala and Live Auction, live music, food and wine, and exclusive chocolate tastings. Demonstrations are also popular. The Wiseman House Fine Chocolates teaches a Chocolate Tempering Demonstration where guests learn how to handle chocolate like a professional. Chocolatiers also demonstrate how to make chocolate set up, a process commonly known as tempering. The Fat Turkey Chocolate Company, meanwhile, educates visitors on the origins of chocolate, the history of chocolate, and chocolate production and manufacturing. The festival concludes with a gourmet black-tie dinner where attendees enjoy five delicious courses of gourmet Texas food and a very special chocolate dessert prepared by the Fat Turkey Chocolate Company. The dinner is an amazing food, wine, and chocolate experience for everyone in attendance.

The Fat Turkey Chocolate Company, incidentally, is an Austin-based business that began when Jennifer Flood and her mother began making chocolate truffles for family and friends. Today, the thriving business helps sponsor the Austin Chocolate Festival while promoting local businesses and raising awareness of breast cancer.

(Austin Chocolate Festival)

Chocolate Crème Brûlée with Blackberries

Adapted from the recipe by Jennifer Flood

Yield: 4 servings

4 oz. semi-sweet chocolate, coarsely chopped	4 large egg yolks
1 cup heavy cream	½ cup granulated sugar
½ cup milk	½ pt. fresh blackberries

1. Preheat the oven to 350°F. Place 4 ramekins in a large roasting pan, and fill the pan with water until it reaches halfway up the ramekins.

2. Place chocolate in a mixing bowl, and place the mixing bowl over a pot with water in it. The bottom of the mixing bowl should not touch water. Bring water to a low simmer over medium heat.

3. In a small saucepan over medium heat, bring cream and milk to a boil. Whisk cream and milk with melted chocolate until smooth. Set aside.

4. In a separate bowl, whisk together egg yolks and ¼ cup sugar until blended, not foamy. Gradually whisk in chocolate mixture until blended.

5. Strain mixture through a fine mesh sieve into a container that pours easily, such as a large glass measuring cup. Pour equal amounts of mixture into the ramekins in the roasting pan, filling them about ¾ full.

6. Carefully transfer the roasting pan to the oven and bake for 30 to 35 minutes or until the center is set. Check for doneness by jiggling the pan. Cool at room temperature and then refrigerate for at least 1 hour.

7. To serve, remove cooled crème brûlée from the refrigerator. Scoop out a little crème brûlée in each dish to make room for blackberries. Nestle 2 or 2 blackberries into each dish.

8. Cover surface of crème brûlée with remaining ¼ cup sugar. Using a plumber's torch, heat sugar until it hardens by slowly moving the flame about ¼ inch above the surface. Sugar should be dark brown to black in color. Be sure to not miss the edges, corners, and blackberries. Serve immediately after torching.

Walnut Cardamom Fudge

Adapted from the recipe by Sara Mayfield

2 oz. unsweetened chocolate	2 TB. butter
2 cups sugar	1 tsp. vanilla extract
⅛ tsp. salt	⅓ cup chopped walnuts
¾ cup milk	1 TB. ground cardamom
2 TB. corn syrup	

1. Oil a 9×9-inch glass pan.

2. In a large pot, combine chocolate, sugar, salt, milk, and corn syrup. Stir constantly over medium-high heat until sugar is dissolved. Reduce heat to medium and cook until mixture reaches the soft boil stage (238°F), stirring frequently.

3. Remove the pot from heat and add butter. Stir until mixture cools to 120°F. Whisk vigorously until mixture begins to harden. Add vanilla extract, walnuts, and cardamom, and mix well.

4. Pour into the prepared pan. Cut into squares before fudge hardens.

Coconut Chocolate Fudge Cake

Adapted from the recipe by Rebecca Rather

Yield: 1 cake

1½ cups unsalted butter	2 cups all-purpose flour
½ cup unsweetened Dutch-process cocoa powder	1 tsp. baking soda
	½ tsp. salt
¼ cup water	2 cups shredded coconut
2 cups sugar	¼ cup whole milk
2 large eggs	½ cup specialty dark cocoa powder
1 cup buttermilk	2 cups sifted confectioners' sugar
3 TB. vanilla extract	

---

1. Preheat the oven to 350°F. Grease and flour a 10- to 12-cup Bundt pan.

2. Melt 1 cup butter in a large saucepan over low heat. Do not boil. Whisk in unsweetened cocoa powder. Whisk in water.

3. Remove the pan from heat and whisk in sugar, eggs, buttermilk, and 2 tablespoons vanilla extract. Add flour, baking soda, ¼ teaspoon salt, and 1 cup shredded coconut. Whisk until all dry ingredients are fully incorporated.

4. Pour batter into the prepared Bundt pan, and bake for 40 to 45 minutes or until cake pulls away from the side of the pan. Let cool and then remove from pan.

5. While cake is baking, melt remaining ½ cup butter in a medium saucepan over low heat. Do not boil. Whisk in whole milk, specialty dark cocoa powder, and confectioners' sugar until glossy.

6. Remove the pan from heat and whisk in remaining 1 tablespoon vanilla extract, remaining ¼ teaspoon salt, and remaining 1 cup shredded coconut.

7. Cover cake with glaze using a spoon. Serve with hand-whipped cream.

Rocky Road Cake

Adapted from the recipe by Betty Hawkins

Yield: 1 cake

2 cups flour	2 eggs, whisked
8 TB. cocoa	1 tsp. baking soda
2 cups sugar	2 tsp. vanilla extract
½ cup buttermilk	1 lb. confectioners' sugar
2½ sticks butter	2 or 3 TB. milk
1 cup water	1 cup chopped and toasted nuts

1. Preheat the oven to 300°F. Grease and flour a 9×13 pan.

2. In a large bowl, mix together flour, 4 tablespoons cocoa, sugar, and buttermilk. Set aside.

3. In a large pan over medium heat, bring 2 sticks butter and water to a boil. Pour into flour mixture and whisk well. Whisk in eggs, baking soda, and 1 teaspoon vanilla extract.

4. Pour into the prepared pan and bake for 30 minutes.

5. While cake bakes, in a large bowl and with a mixer on medium to medium-high speed, blend together remaining ½ stick softened butter, remaining 4 tablespoons cocoa, confectioners' sugar, milk, remaining 1 teaspoon vanilla extract, and nuts.

6. Remove cake from the oven and ice while cake is hot. Wait for cake to cool, cover, and refrigerate. Serve cold with ice cream.

Fourteen-Hour Pork Mole Taco

Adapted from the recipe by Jeff Holberg

2 to 4 lb. pork butts	3 TB. chopped garlic
Cajun seasoning	1 tsp. dried oregano
Salt and pepper	1 tsp. ground cumin
Garlic salt	¼ tsp. ground cinnamon
4 TB. olive oil plus more as needed (not extra virgin)	2½ TB. chili powder
	3 TB. all-purpose flour
¼ cup water	4½ cups chicken broth
1 cup finely chopped onion	2 oz. semi-sweet chocolate, chopped

1. Preheat the oven to 350°F to 400°F.

2. Season pork with Cajun seasoning, salt, pepper, and garlic salt, pressing seasoning into meat.

3. Heat a cast-iron Dutch oven over medium-high heat. Add 1 tablespoon olive oil or just enough to cover the bottom of the pot. Add pork and brown both sides.

4. Remove pork and set aside. Deglaze the Dutch oven with water, scraping the bottom.

5. Place pork back in the Dutch oven, and add water until meat is almost all covered. Cover and bake for 1 to 1½ hours.

6. Remove from the oven, place pork in a shallow pan, and shred pork using a fork. Add ½ cup juice from the Dutch oven to shredded pork to help keep it moist.

7. While pork is cooking, heat remaining 3 tablespoons olive oil in a large saucepan over medium-low heat. Add onion, garlic, oregano, cumin, and cinnamon. Cover and cook until onion is almost tender, stirring occasionally, about 10 minutes. Mix in chili powder and flour, and stir for 3 minutes. Gradually whisk in chicken broth.

8. Increase heat to medium-high, and boil until reduced, about 35 minutes, stirring occasionally.

9. Remove the pan from heat. Whisk in chocolate, and season with salt and pepper, if desired.

10. To serve, place shredded pork in a warm flour tortilla and top with heated mole sauce.

Note: Not all chocolate dishes are desserts. Here's a popular recipe featured at the Austin Chocolate Festival. These tacos are so popular, the festival always seems to run out.

CHOCOLATE LOVERS FESTIVAL

Fairfax, Virginia
February
703-385-1661
www.chocolatefestival.net

With chocolate so popular with dessert lovers, it's only fitting that a second chocolate festival be featured. And what a festival it is! The Chocolate Lovers Festival in Fairfax, Virginia, is a festival for serious cocoa connoisseurs, featuring activities for all ages to enjoy.

In 1992, the Chocolate Lovers Festival was created to draw chocolate lovers around the region into the Old Town of Fairfax. Since its inception, the famous festival continues its annual tradition of showcasing the "love of chocolate" as its central theme.

This 2-day festival held each February includes a long list of chocolate vendors, an arts extravaganza using chocolate as the medium, a pancake breakfast featuring chocolate-chip pancakes, and a Crafts Show and Bake Sale offering endless items featuring delicious chocolate. There's also a Chocolate Challenge where professionals and amateurs alike create marvelous chocolate cakes and sculptures. These winning creations are available for bidding at a silent auction that follows. The Taste of Chocolate, on the other hand, is probably one of the most popular events at the festival, where visitors surround themselves with hundreds of the finest chocolate sensations, including chocolate cakes, candies, brownies, fudge, ice cream, and other delicious chocolate surprises.

Chocolate has been around for centuries. History books claim chocolate was developed by the early Mayan and Aztec civilizations, who cultivated cacao beans and produced various chocolates that were used as a main ingredient in a variety of sauces and beverages. Today, true, genuine chocolate is made from the fermented, roasted, and ground beans taken from the pod of the tropical cacao tree, native to Central America and Mexico. As chocolate production increased, so did the planting of cacao trees, which can now be found throughout the tropical regions of the world.

(*Chocolate Lovers Festival*)

Martha Washington's Colonial Chocolate

Adapted from the recipe by the Chocolate Lovers Festival

Yield: 6 servings

4 TB. cocoa	2 TB. cornstarch
2 cups water	1 egg
⅓ cup sugar	½ cup hot water
2 cups milk	½ tsp. vanilla extract

1. Combine cocoa in a small amount of cold water in a saucepan over medium-high heat, and mix to a smooth paste. Stir in 2 cups water, sugar, and milk. Bring to a boil, and blend in cornstarch that's been dissolved in a little bit of cold milk. Boil 3 minutes longer, remove from heat, and set in a warm place.

2. Beat egg and hot water until light and foamy. Pour ½ egg mixture into a pitcher, and blend in vanilla extract. Add cocoa mixture slowly.

3. Pour remaining egg mixture over top, and serve at once.

Chocolate Truffles

Adapted from the recipe by Tina Cunningham

Yield: 40 pieces or 1½ pounds

1 (12-oz.) pkg. semi-sweet chocolate chips	1 tsp. vanilla extract
	Pinch salt
¾ cup sweetened condensed milk	¾ cup pistachios, coarsely chopped

1. In a double boiler over hot but not boiling water, melt chocolate chips. Remove from heat.

2. Stir in condensed milk, vanilla extract, and salt until well mixed.

3. Refrigerate about 30 minutes or until mixture is easy to shape. With buttered hands, shape mixture into 1-inch balls and roll in pistachios. Store truffles in a tightly covered container in a cool place.

Chocolate and Strawberry–Filled French Toast

Adapted from the recipe by the Chocolate Lovers Festival

Yield: 2 servings

2 (1-in.-thick) diagonal slices of day-old French bread

¼ cup mini chocolate chips

1¼ cups strawberry preserves

2 TB. cream cheese, softened

2 eggs, lightly beaten

¼ cup milk

¼ cup sugar

½ tsp. vanilla extract

Dash cinnamon

Confectioners' sugar

¼ cup apricot preserves

1 small can mandarin oranges, drained

3 TB. butter, for frying

¼ cup butter, melted

1. Cut through each slice of bread horizontally to form a pocket, not cutting all the way through. Stuff ⅛ cup chocolate chips and ⅛ cup strawberry preserves into each pocket along with 1 tablespoon softened cream cheese.

2. In a shallow bowl, whisk together eggs, milk, sugar, vanilla extract, and cinnamon. Add filled bread to the bowl and allow to soak for 5 to 10 minutes.

3. In a heavy skillet or griddle, heat 3 tablespoons butter until foam subsides. Add bread, turning frequently until crisp and golden. Transfer toast to heated plates and dust with confectioners' sugar. Keep warm.

4. In a saucepan over low heat, add remaining 1 cup strawberry preserves, apricot preserves, mandarin oranges, and butter, and stir until well blended. Serve Mandarin Orange Strawberry Sauce over warm french toast.

Ridiculously Easy Chocolate Cake

Adapted from the recipe by Mandy Brook

Yield: 1 cake

2 cups sugar	1 cup whole milk, rice, or soy milk
1¾ cups flour	½ cup vegetable oil
¾ cup cocoa	1 tsp. vanilla extract
½ tsp. baking powder	1 tsp. almond extract
½ tsp. baking soda	1 cup boiling water
1 tsp. salt	Confectioners' sugar
2 eggs	

---

1. Preheat the oven to 350°F. Grease a Bundt pan and dust with cocoa.

2. In a large bowl, combine sugar, flour, cocoa, baking powder, baking soda, and salt. Add eggs, milk, vegetable oil, vanilla extract, and almond extract, and beat until thoroughly mixed. Stir in boiling water.

3. Pour batter into the prepared pan and bake 35 to 40 minutes or until toothpick inserted into highest point comes out clean.

4. Cool on wire rack and turn upside down onto serving a plate. Dust with confectioners' sugar just before serving.

ATTENDING A FOOD FESTIVAL

Comparable to a trip to the fairgrounds or an amusement park, visiting a food festival is a fun-filled celebration geared toward the entire family. From the small, serene Ponca City Herb Festival in Oklahoma to one of the largest food festivals in the United States—the Gilroy Garlic Festival in California—American food festivals are culinary vacations and indulgent escapes, both for your taste buds and your wallet. Expect to find delicious food, interactive cooking demonstrations, wildly exciting eating competitions, hours of musical entertainment, and plenty of fun and games for the kids at many of America's greatest food festivals. If you've been longing for a weekend focused on decadent food and food-related activities, consider attending a food festival, where you'll not only eat well, but also get to observe local tradition and culture up close and personal through the common language of food.

(Great American Pie Festival)

LOCATING THE PERFECT FESTIVAL

In the United States today, food festivals are held every month of the year in every state in the country. While there may be only three or four festivals taking place in locales such as Alaska, Hawaii, Washington, and some of the smaller states, states such as California, Florida, and Texas boast upward of 20 to 30 food festivals per year.

Without question, this book is a great reference and starting guide to locate the perfect festival for you, but probably your best bet for uncovering the ideal festival is researching online. While browsing the web, you'll quickly discover that there's a festival for virtually every kind of food, from grits, pumpkins, and hot dogs, to oysters, ice cream, and tofu. Like planning a family vacation, study each festival website to learn more about the event, what month to travel, associated costs and attractions, and exactly what is offered and what is not.

No access to a computer? Simply contact the tourism board or chamber of commerce in the state you're thinking of visiting. Every state has an office with members who should be happy to assist you with providing the details of their upcoming food festivals. With careful planning, such gastronomic excursions can be enjoyed on any budget.

FOOD FESTIVAL EXPECTATIONS

If there's one definitive expectation at a food festival, it's to expect an overabundance of marvelous food. Definitely come hungry, as each food festival is designed to showcase—what else?—the state's most cherished food. If you find yourself getting tired of eating nothing but cornbread, clams, or SPAM, many festivals invite neighboring food vendors to serve up plenty of nonfestival fare. As they say, variety is the spice of life, and this is aptly expressed at every American food festival today.

Not a particular fan of long lines or occupied tables? Then perhaps a large food festival isn't for you. Many of the country's most famous festivals, like the Gilroy Garlic Festival in California or the National Peanut Festival in Alabama, are national attractions that welcome tens of thousands of visitors over multiple days. Similar in experience to an outing at Disney World or a big ballgame, plenty of noise, controlled chaos, and limited elbow room are all part of the celebratory atmosphere.

Conversely, many of the smaller festivals, like the Potato Days Festival in Minnesota or the Horseradish Festival in Illinois, pride themselves on entertaining the local community with old-fashioned entertainment. Far removed from the confines of a big city, such festivals often include free admission and simple concessions, as they just don't have the staff or resources to handle the enormous crowds.

Cost of Admission

The cost of attending a food festival varies, often determined by the size and venue of the festival. Many food festivals are free to the public, while other festivals charge an admission fee as well as tickets to accompanying events and musical acts. But unlike attending a professional sporting event, where a single ticket may run as high as $50 or more, food festival admission is extremely affordable—often around $5 or $10 per ticket.

Regardless of the admission price, it's not the entrance fee you should worry about but the endless array of food booths and food-related products available for sale inside. Be sure to budget accordingly and take as much as you're willing to spend. Also, the larger festivals often take major credit cards, but the smaller festivals may operate on a cash-only basis.

Duration of a Food Festival

Depending on the particular festival you plan on attending, most are a one-day event or a two-, three-, or four-day celebration. The National Peanut Festival in Alabama happens to be a 10-day affair. Unless your favorite musician is performing on a particular day or you're scheduled for a cook-off or baking competition, generally one full day at a festival is plenty of time for you to experience and learn everything you would like to know about a particular food.

Food Festival Tips and Pointers

The following is some tried-and-true "insider" advice on making your food festival experience the best it can be:

- Make note of where you parked, particularly if you're in a congested lot or field. After hours at a festival, it's amazing how quickly you forget where your car is.

- Wear comfortable shoes, especially at the larger festivals, where walking is the primary mode of transportation.

- If need be, find out if the festival is wheelchair accessible prior to your arrival.

- Strollers are often permitted inside festival grounds but sometimes present challenges when navigating through grass, wood chips, or dirt pathways. Plan accordingly.

- Have cash on hand (assorted small bills). Some festivals may not take your VISA or appreciate breaking $100 bills.

- Keep a roll of TUMS or an antacid in your pocket or purse to relieve heartburn from overeating.

- Keep hydrated by drinking plenty of water throughout the day.

- During hot summer days at a festival, don't forget your sunscreen, sunglasses, and a hat or visor to protect yourself from the sun.

- Shirts and shoes are required at most, if not all, the festivals.

- Many festivals prohibit bringing certain items into festival grounds, such as alcohol, bottles, glass, nonfestival food, bicycles, skateboards, rollerblades, coolers, chairs, tables, and weapons. Check with the particular festival prior to your arrival.

- Festivals often prohibit dogs and other animals from being brought into the festival. Guide dogs, Seeing Eye dogs, and service dogs are usually permitted. Again, check with the festival prior to your arrival.

PARTICIPATING IN A COOK-OFF OR BAKE-OFF

For you home cooks out there who have dreamed of entering a prized recipe in a food festival, now's your chance for instant fame and recognition.

To begin, find the appropriate festival for your famous dish. If it's an apple cobbler and you live in Wisconsin, you'd best enter it in the Bayfield Apple Festival and not the Florida Citrus Festival, as most festivals only feature recipes that include their featured food.

Next, go online or contact the festival representative to learn the specific submission process. Often, food festivals begin by accepting applications from interested participants months before the event. The application will also spell out the specific rules and regulations. Read the print carefully. Some festivals may only accept applications from folks residing in the state where the festival is held. Others may only accept applications from amateur cooks.

Once you submit your application, the waiting begins. Most festivals select a group of finalist and invite them to the festival to prepare their recipes in front of the general public and a panel of judges. (Refer to the specific festival for competition details.)

The recipes are prepared, presented, and judged by a panel, and winners are chosen. Some festivals offer cash prizes while others give away kitchen gadgets and trophies. Regardless of the awards handed out, it seems the instant fame and culinary recognition is what most cooking participants appreciate most.

PARTICIPATING IN AN EATING CONTEST

Eating competitions are always an exciting venue at food festivals. Competitors line up in anticipation of consuming far more food than ever imagined. For spectators, watching a guy or gal choke down 44 lobsters, 65 hard-boiled eggs, or 247 jalapeño peppers in a matter of minutes is a sight to be seen. In fact, the International Federation of Competitive Eating (IFOCE) monitors many of the eating competitions around the country and keeps track of the world records. (For a complete list of records broken down by food category, log on to www.ifoce.com.)

Of course, not all eating contests are geared toward the professional eater. Many food festivals invite attending adults and children to participate in a chow-down contest. Pie eating is extremely popular and always a hit with the crowd. For specific festival eating contests, contact the particular food festival for rules and regulations prior to arriving.

100 OTHER FUN FESTIVALS

These food festivals, arranged by state, are some of the many diverse festivals you'll find throughout the country. Some are small, communal events orchestrated by a handful of volunteers; others are large, state-run celebrations. Regardless of their size or method of operation, one constant remains throughout the festivals: plenty of delicious food.

For detailed information about each festival, please contact the festival directly or visit them on the web.

Baldwin County Strawberry Festival
Loxley, Alabama
April
www.baldwincountystrawberryfestival.org

Franklin County Watermelon Festival
Russellville, Alabama
August
www.franklincountychamber.org/festival.html

Kodiak Crab Festival
Kodiak Island, Alaska
May
www.kodiak.org/crabfest.html

Grand Canyon Sweet Onion Festival
Gilbert, Arizona
May
www.sweetonionfestival.com

Yuma Lettuce Days
Yuma, Arizona
January
www.yumalettucedays.com

Alma Spinach Festival
Alma, Arkansas
April
almachamber.com/spinachfestival

Arkansas Apple Festival
Lincoln, Arkansas
October
www.arkansasapplefestival.org

Holtville Rib Cook-Off
Holtville, California
January
holtville.net

National Date Festival
Indio, California
February
www.datefest.org

San Francisco Crab Festival
San Francisco, California
February
onlysf.sfvisitor.org/crab_festival

California Peach Festival
Marysville, California
July
www.capeachfestival.com

Santa Cruz Clam Chowder Cook-Off
Santa Cruz, California
February
www.ci.santa-cruz.ca.us/pr/parksrec/events/
special.html

Oxnard Salsa Festival
Oxnard, California
July
www.oxnardsalsafestival.com

Olathe Sweet Corn Festival
Olathe, Colorado
August
www.olathesweetcornfest.com

The Rocky Mountain Tea Festival
Boulder, Colorado
August
www.boulderteahouse.com/teafest.html

Mystic Seaport Lobster Days
Mystic, Connecticut
May
www.mysticseaport.org

Stonington Vineyards Wine and Food Festival
Stonington, Connecticut
May, July, September
www.stoningtonvineyards.com

Dover Downs Wine and Music Festival
Dover Downs, Delaware
November
www.doverdownswinefest.com

Everglades Seafood Festival
Everglades City, Florida
February
www.evergladesseafoodfestival.com

Palm Beach Seafood Festival
West Palm Beach, Florida
March
www.fantasma.com/special

Stone Crab, Seafood and Wine Festival
Longboat Key, Florida
October
www.colonybeachresort.com/stonecrab/index.
html

Delray Beach Garlic Fest
Delray Beach, Florida
February
www.dbgarlicfest.com

Vidalia Onion Festival
Vidalia, Georgia
April
www.vidaliaonionfestival.com

Wild Georgia Shrimp Festival
Jekyll Island, Georgia
September
www.jekyllisland.com/shrimpandgrits

Taste of Honolulu
Honolulu, Hawaii
June
www.taste808.com

Kona Chocolate Festival
Kona, Hawaii
March
www.konachocolatefestival.com

Emmett Cherry Festival
Emmett, Idaho
June
www.emmettidaho.com

Raspberry Festival
Cottonwood, Idaho
August
www.historicalmuseumatstgertrude.com/
Events/musrasfest.html

All Things Organic
Chicago, Illinois
May
www.organicexpo.com

All Candy Expo
Chicago, Illinois
September
www.allcandyexpo.com

The Strawberry Festival
Crawfordsville, Indiana
June
www.thestrawberryfestival.com

Marshall County Blueberry Festival
Plymouth, Indiana
September
www.blueberryfestival.org

West Point Sweet Corn Festival
West Point, Iowa
August
www.westpointcornfestival.com

Chili and Salsa Cook-Off
Sioux City, Iowa
September
www.downtownsiouxcity.com/chilicook-off.
html

Flint Hills Beef Fest
Emporia, Kansas
August
www.geocities.com/beeffest

Lenexa Spinach Festival
Lenexa, Kansas
September
www.ci.lenexa.ks.us/parks/spinachfestival.
html

Burnside Catfish Festival
Burnside, Kentucky
September
www.burnsideky.org/catfish.php

World Chicken Festival
London, Kentucky
September
www.chickenfestival.com

Ponchatoula Strawberry Festival
Ponchatoula, Louisiana
April
www.lastrawberryfestival.com

Delcambre Shrimp Festival
Delcambre, Louisiana
August
www.shrimpfestival.net

ChiliFest
Wells, Maine
September
www.wellschamber.org/events.htm

Baltimore Crab and Beer Festival
Baltimore, Maryland
September
www.mdcrabfest.com

St. Mary's County Oyster Festival
St. Mary's County, Maryland
October
www.usoysterfest.com

Fisherman's Feast
Boston, Massachusetts
August
www.fishermansfeast.com

Cape Cod BBQ Challenge
Hyannis, Massachusetts
June
www.capecodchallenge.com

Wellfleet OysterFest
Wellfleet, Massachusetts
October
www.wellfleetoysterfest.org

Battle Creek Cereal Festival
Battle Creek, Michigan
June
www.cerealfest.com

Cheeseburger in Caseville
Caseville, Michigan
August
www.cheeseburgerincaseville.com

Rhubarb Festival
Lanesboro, Minnesota
June
www.lanesboro.com/rhubarbfestival/index.
php

Minnesota Food and Wine Festival
Alexandria, Minnesota
September
www.carloscreekwinery.com

Biloxi Seafood Festival
Biloxi, Mississippi
September
www.biloxi.org

Mississippi Coast Coliseum Crawfish Festival
Biloxi, Mississippi
April
www.mscoastcoliseum.com/event_
crawfishfest.htm

Mushroom Festival
Richmond, Missouri
May
cofcommerce.home.mchsi.com/festival.html

Rock'n Ribs BBQ Festival
Springfield, Missouri
April
www.rocknribs.com

Rocky Mountain Oyster Festival
Clinton, Montana
September
www.testyfesty.com

AppleJack Festival
Nebraska City, Nebraska
September
www.nebraskacity.com/ajack.html

Taste of Omaha
Omaha, Nebraska
June
www.showofficeonline.com/Taste/index.htm

World Tea Expo
Las Vegas, Nevada
June
www.takeme2tea.com

Hearts O' Gold Cantaloupe Festival
Fallon, Nevada
September
www.fallontourism.com/media/hearts.o.gold.
html

Best in the West Nugget Rib Cook-Off
Sparks, Nevada
August/September
www.nuggetribcookoff.com

Pumpkin Festival
Keene, New Hampshire
October
www.pumpkinfestival.org

Shad Festival
Lambertville, New Jersey
April
www.lambertville.org

New Jersey Fresh Seafood Festival
Atlantic City, New Jersey
June
www.njfreshseafoodfest.com

The Cranberry Festival of Chatsworth
Chatsworth, New Jersey
October
www.cranfest.org

National Fiery-Foods and Barbecue Show
Albuquerque, New Mexico
March
www.fiery-foods.com/shows.asp

Santa Fe Wine and Chile Fiesta
Santa Fe, New Mexico
September
www.santafewineandchile.org

Taste of Chinatown
New York, New York
October
www.explorechinatown.com

Taste of New York
Sackets Harbor, New York
July
www.tasteofnewyorkmarket.com

Pig Cookin' Contest
Newport, North Carolina
March
www.newportpigcooking.com

North Carolina Watermelon Festival
Fair Bluff, North Carolina
July
www.ncwatermelonfestival.com

Milan Melon Festival
Milan, Ohio
September
www.accnorwalk.com/MelonFestival

Beavercreek Popcorn Festival
Beavercreek, Ohio
September
Beavercreek.hcst.net/popcorn

Elephant Garlic Festival
North Plains, Oregon
August
www.funstinks.com

Sutherlin Blackberry Festival
Sutherlin, Oregon
August
www.sutherlinbbfest.org

Bite of Oregon
Waterfront Park, Oregon
August
www.biteoforegon.com

Pennsylvania Maple Festival
Meyersdale, Pennsylvania
March/April
www.pamaplefestival.com

Mushroom Festival
Kennett Square, Pennsylvania
September
www.mushroomfestival.org

Chili Pepper Food Festival
Bowers, Pennsylvania
September
www.pepperfestival.com

Great Chowder Cook-Off
Newport, Rhode Island
June
www.newportfestivals.com/Chowder-Cook-Off

Pageland Watermelon Festival
Pageland, South Carolina
July
www.pagelandchamber.com

Okra Strut Festival
Irmo, South Carolina
September
www.irmookrastrut.com

Great Plains Bison-Tennial Dutch Oven Cook-Off
Yankton, South Dakota
August
www.dutchovencookoff.com

Tennessee Soybean Festival
Martin, Tennessee
September
www.tnsoybeanfestival.org

Tomato Art Fest
Nashville, Tennessee
August
www.tomatoartfest.com

West Tennessee Strawberry Festival
Dayton, Tennessee
May
www.wtsf.org

Oysterfest
Fulton, Texas
March
www.fultontexas.org/oysterfest.html

Texas Steak Cook-Off
Hico, Texas
July
www.texassteakcookoff.com

Poteet Strawberry Festival
Poteet, Texas
April
www.strawberryfestival.com

Vermont Maple Festival
St. Albans, Vermont
April
www.vtmaplefestival.org

Green Mountain Chew Chew Festival
Burlington, Vermont
June
www.greenmountainchewchew.com

Chocolate Lovers Festival
Fairfax, Virginia
February
www.chocolatefestival.net

Charlottesville Vegetarian Festival
Charlottesville, Virginia
September
www.cvillevegfest.org

Penn Cove Mussel Festival
Whidbey Island, Washington
March
www.penncovemusselfestival.com

Wild Mushroom Celebration
Long Beach, Washington
October
www.funbeach.com/mushroom/index.html

Seattle Cheese Festival
Seattle, Washington
May
www.seattlecheesefestival.com

National Capital Barbecue Battle
Washington, D.C.
June
www.bbqusa.us

Buckwheat Festival
Kingwood, West Virginia
September
www.prestoncounty.com/pcbf.htm

West Virginia Strawberry Festival
Buckhannon, West Virginia
May
www.wvstrawberryfestival.com

Warrens Cranberry Festival
Warrens, Wisconsin
September
www.cranfest.com

Strawberry Festival
Cedarburg, Wisconsin
June
www.cedarburgfestivals.org/Strawberry.html

INDEX

C

G

H

O

P

Q–R